PRAISE FOR *REDUCE CHANG INCREASE IMPROVEMENT*

There are many reasons Viviane Robinson is one of my favorite researchers in the field of educational leadership. Her depth of knowledge and understanding of school improvement make her a standout in the profession. *Reduce Change to Increase Improvement* is a book all leaders should read because it will help them understand what improvement looks like and how to avoid the pitfalls that too many leaders fall into.

Peter DeWitt, EdD, Corwin Author/Consultant
Finding Common Ground blog (*Education Week*)
Albany, NY

Viviane Robinson's brilliant new masterpiece is provocatively titled *Reduce Change to Increase Improvement*. It is a stunning achievement. Every sentence bristles with penetrating insights and practical recommendations in the hands of Robinson's sparkling prose. The sections on engaging respectfully with teachers' theories of action should be required reading for every school principal or superintendent. Best of all, this expertly crafted book is a pleasure to read and re-read. It will be cited frequently around the world for years to come.

Dennis Shirley, Professor
Lynch School of Education, Boston College
Chestnut Hill, MA

Finally, a serious, evidence-proven book about educational change that takes a different tack—beginning with the impact on the learner. *Reduce Change to Increase Improvement* is a treasure trove of concrete information for educational leaders wanting to move away from the frequently used, ineffective Bypass Theory leading to no change in student outcomes to the rarely used, highly effective Engagement Theory that gets at the heart of leading school improvement. Robinson, always cautious about "change for change's sake," brilliantly delineates each step of the way for leaders using authentically documented conversations and practical discussion starters that guide us through this collective inquiry approach toward student improvement. She highlights that only by integrating new thinking into current classroom practice will reform be successful—AND only if built on a firm foundation of leaders and teachers rigorously examining shared beliefs and exposing tacitly held disbeliefs about the capacity of all students to learn. All leaders need this concise, clearly stated text to guide their intentional improvement practices.

Dr. Lyn Sharratt, International Consultant and Author
OISE, University of Toronto
Toronto, ON

This is a "must read" for anyone who is serious about achieving meaningful improvement and understanding more about the potential of engaging with theories of action. With her forensic eye for detail, Viviane Robinson unpicks why current practice is sustained and shows how deep and respectful coaching dialogue can produce mutual commitment and powerful professional learning. It's a book with many applications.

Louise Stoll, Ph.D., Professor of Professional Learning
London Centre for Leadership in Learning/
UCL Institute of Education
London, England

Never was a book more welcome than one that addresses why so much change leads to so little impact. Viviane's work gets right to the heart of the beliefs, values, and conditions that lie at the heart of our willingness to either embrace change or resist it. She lays bare the actions of leaders who are passionate advocates of reform, but all too often end up with disappointing results. She gives us an opportunity to eavesdrop on real conversations that model skillful enquiry into the values and beliefs that drive our behaviour and that are more likely to lead to change that "pays off." The book both advocates and models enquiry, and the questions posed at the end of each chapter are insightful and powerful. In a world where change is constant and resources are tight, we should all be intolerant of any more failed attempts. I would like to see every Education Ministry, school adviser, and school leader not just reading this book but using it to shape their practice so change can be far less frequent, but have far more impact.

Maggie Farrar, Education Consultant
FarrarChapman Ltd
Formerly interim CEO and Director of Research and Policy at the
National College for School Leadership, England

Viviane Robinson has once again managed to connect research and practice in a way that both makes the readers trust her conclusions and gives them concrete ideas of how to enhance school improvement work. "Reduce Change to Increase Improvement" is a powerful contribution to school leaders who have the ambition of making a difference for their schools.

Omar Mekki, Senior Advisor
The IMTEC Foundation
Oslo, Norway

My colleague Dr. Judy Halbert and I have worked with principals in graduate programs and in professional learning series in six countries over the last two decades. Each and every one of these leaders would benefit from reading this new book by Professor Robinson. She combines her research findings, a logic train that is important and highly usable, a powerful insight into how to redesign thinking about principal well-being and work load, and examples from practice that are invaluable. Her writing has voice and is highly engaging to read. The sooner this book has been published, the better. These theoretically powerful and practical insights are needed and overdue.

Dr. Linda Kaser, Co-Director of the Center for Innovative
Educational Leadership
Transformational Educational Leadership Program, UBC
Vancouver, BC

The challenge in our current understanding of school improvement is not knowing what schools ought to do, but knowing how school leaders can get those things done. Leaders' ability to engage and involve teachers in improvement processes is a missing resource in many schools. Reading this book will absolutely help school leaders redefine how they should act and behave in order to implement improvements to benefit not only their students' learning but also teachers' professional development. This book makes a significant contribution to the education management literature in a clear, concise and practical way. A "must read" for new and established school leaders.

Johan From, Professor in Political Science/Director of School Leadership Master's Program
BI Norwegian Business School
Oslo, Norway

This book is remarkable. It combines a deep understanding of how and why theories of action influence the success or failure of improvement efforts in schools, with a range of intensely practical strategies and examples that illustrate how leaders can work to enhance their approaches to change. Robinson draws on more than 10 years of research and development work with leaders, often based on detailed observation and analysis of coaching conversations and real situations in schools, to identify and make explicit the values, beliefs, actions and consequences that drive behavior and the ways in which leaders can engage with these to create shared understandings and agendas for improvement. The chapter on how this work informed the design of a new leadership development program to address well-being for school principals is particularly fascinating. I can't recommend the book highly enough to serving leaders and all those involved in supporting change and improvement in schools.

Toby Greany, Professor
London Centre for Leadership in Learning
London, England

In her new book, Professor Viviane Robinson provides school leaders with tools and even conversational scripts to move their schools through an improvement process. The knowledge school leaders will gain from this book will help them reframe resistance to change and guide them in helping implementers openly engage in evaluating the relative merits of existing and proposed school processes. This book is a wonderful resource for school leaders in navigating school improvement successfully.

Professor Darleen Opfer, Director
RAND Education
Washington, D.C.

Reduce Change to Increase Improvement

Corwin Impact Leadership Series

Series Editor: Peter M. DeWitt

Reaching the Heart of Leadership: Lessons Learned, Insights Gained, Actions Taken by Avis Glaze

Indelible Leadership: Always Leave Them Learning by Michael Fullan

Principal Voice: Listen, Learn, Lead by Russell J. Quaglia

Reduce Change to Increase Improvement by Viviane Robinson

FinnishED Leadership: Four Big, Inexpensive Ideas to Transform Education by Pasi Sahlberg

Teaching for Greatness: Learner-Driven Education by Yong Zhao

And a forthcoming contribution from Andy Hargreaves

Reduce Change to Increase Improvement

Viviane Robinson

Corwin Impact Leadership Series

Series Editor: Peter M. DeWitt

CORWIN
A SAGE Publishing Company

FOR INFORMATION:

Corwin

A SAGE Company

2455 Teller Road

Thousand Oaks, California 91320

(800) 233-9936

www.corwin.com

SAGE Publications Ltd.

1 Oliver's Yard

55 City Road

London EC1Y 1SP

United Kingdom

SAGE Publications India Pvt. Ltd.

B 1/I 1 Mohan Cooperative Industrial Area

Mathura Road, New Delhi 110 044

India

SAGE Publications Asia-Pacific Pte. Ltd.

3 Church Street

#10-04 Samsung Hub

Singapore 049483

Printed in the United States of America

ISBN: 978-1-5063-2537-8

This book is printed on acid-free paper.

Executive Editor: Arnis Burvikovs

Senior Associate Editor: Desirée A. Bartlett

Editorial Assistant: Kaitlyn Irwin

Production Editor: Andrew Olson

Copy Editor: Jared Leighton

Typesetter: C&M Digitals (P) Ltd.

Proofreader: Liann Lech

Indexer: Molly Hall

Cover Designer: Michael Dubowe

17 18 19 20 21 10 9 8 7 6 5 4 3 2 1

Contents

List of Tables and Figures   xiii

Preface   xv

Acknowledgments   xix

About the Author   xxi

1. Too Much Change, Not Enough Improvement   1

    Not All Change Is Desirable   2

    Distinguish Between Change and Improvement   3

       The Distinction Between Change and Improvement
       Increases Leaders' Accountability   3

       The Distinction Fosters Vigilance About Whether
       Change Is Working   5

       Is the Change Worth It?   5

    Improvement Means Positive Impact on Learners   6

    The Impact of Leadership on Student Outcomes   8

    Reflection and Action   12

2. Understand the Challenge of Improvement   13

    Understand Theories of Action   14

    Espoused Theories of Action Versus
       Theories in Use   17

    Helping to Change Theories of Action   20

    Reflection and Action   22

3. Two Approaches to Leading Improvement:
   Bypass and Engage 25

   The Limitations of the Bypass Approach 28
    Double-Loop Learning Is Unlikely 28
    Too Little Critical Scrutiny of the Alternative Theory 29
    Bypass May Produce Mutual Mistrust 29
   The Bypass Approach: A National Initiative 30
   From Bypass to Engagement 32
    From Bypass to Engagement: A School Initiative 33
   Reflection and Action 35

4. The Four Phases of Theory Engagement 37

   Phase I. Agree on the Problem to Be Solved 38
    Data Can Suggest What Is Problematic 40
    Constructive Problem Talk 40
    Defensive Problem Talk 43
    Gain Sufficient Agreement 45
   Phase II. Inquire Into the Relevant Theory of Action 45
    Ask Direct and Respectful Questions 46
    Postpone Evaluation of the Theory 49
    Inquire Systematically Into Each Component
     of the Theory of Action 50
   Phase III. Evaluate the Relative Merit of the Current
    and Alternative Theories of Action 55
    Which Values Are Important? 56
    Theory Evaluation and Interpersonal Behavior 59
    Communicating Respectful Evaluations 62
   Phase IV. Implement and Monitor a New, Sufficiently
    Shared Theory of Action 64
    Use Implementation and Outcome Indicators 64
    Embed the Indicators in the Work of Improvement 66
   Reflection and Action 69

5. Learning How to Lead Improvement: Coaching
   That Engages Principals 71

   Excerpt 1: Engage Others' Thinking 72
    Layer 1: The Coach Brings Relevant Knowledge 77
    Layer 2: The Coach Models How to Maintain
     a Shared Focus 77

Layer 3: The Coach Enacts the Interpersonal
Values of Respect, Truth-Seeking, and
Internal Commitment   78
Excerpt 2: The Self-Referential Critique   79
How to Provide Self-Referential Critique   82
Excerpt 3: Bypass and Reframing   82
Reflection and Action   86

6. Learning How to Lead Improvement: Professional
Learning That Engages Participants   87

The Context   89
Phase I. Agree on the Problem to Be Solved   91
Phase II. Reveal the Relevant Theories of Action   93
Construct a General Theory of Action   93
Construct a Personal Theory of Action   96
Phase III. Evaluate the Relative Merit of the Current
and Alternative Theories of Action   98
Construct and Evaluate an Alternative General
Theory of Action   98
Phase IV. Implement and Monitor a New, Sufficiently
Shared Theory of Action   102
Reflection and Action   108

Afterword by Stephen Dinham   109

References   111

Index   115

List of Tables and Figures

Figure 1.1	Average Effects of Five Dimensions of Educational Leadership on Student Outcomes	10
Figure 2.1	The Structure of a Theory of Action	15
Figure 2.2	A Comparison Between Claudia's Current and Possible Future Theory of Action for Teaching Math	16
Figure 2.3	Two Types of Theories of Action	18
Figure 2.4	Single- and Double-Loop Learning	21
Figure 3.1	The Bypass and Engage Approaches to Leading Improvement	26
Figure 4.1	The Four Phases of Theory Engagement	39
Table 4.1	Constructive Problem Talk	42
Table 4.2	Direct and Respectful Inquiry Into a Theory of Action	47
Table 4.3	Systematic and Responsive Inquiry Into a Theory of Action	51
Figure 4.2	John's Theory of Action for Helping Pam	54
Figure 4.3	Two Forms of Bypass in the Communication of Critical Evaluations	60
Figure 4.4	From Bypass to Engage in the Communication of Critical Evaluations	62

Table 4.4	Direct and Respectful Evaluation of a Theory of Action	63
Figure 4.5	An Alternative Theory of Action for the Teaching of Recount Writing	68
Table 5.1	Analysis of Excerpt 1	75
Table 5.2	Analysis of Excerpt 2	81
Table 5.3	Analysis of Excerpt 3	85
Figure 6.1	A General Theory of Action for Principals' Time Use	94
Figure 6.2	A Personal Theory of Action for One Principal's Time Use	97
Figure 6.3	A General Alternative Theory of Action for Principals' Time Use	99
Figure 6.4	An Alternative Personal Theory of Action for One Principal's Time Use	101
Table 6.1	A Course Design for Engaging Participants' Theory of Action	103

Preface

The practical purpose of this book is to help system and school leaders to increase improvement while reducing ineffective change and innovation. Whether change is thrust upon them or pursued through their own choice, I want to help leaders increase its payoff so that planned change is undertaken less frequently and, when it is, more successfully. It is time to stop talking about change and to focus on the far more ambitious goal of achieving improvement.

Planned changes often fail because those designing them underestimate the complexity of implementation—a complexity that is experienced by implementing agents but given too little attention by change leaders. In this book, I ask questions and offer answers about why this ineffective approach to change happens so often and how it can be interrupted and transformed. My focus is on the ***process by which change is led*** and on how and why change advocates fail to learn what is involved in achieving their ambitions. By drilling down to the beliefs and values that inform the actual practice of change leaders, I identify the thinking, the processes, and the actual behaviors that contribute to failed reform efforts and, importantly, provide them with concrete tools that enable them to be more effective. Those tools go well beyond the usual abstract descriptions of the four or five key principles or action steps that are urged upon change leaders. They link the ethics of change leadership to a clear change process, and that process is richly illustrated in ways that answer questions about what to do and what to say.

The standard to which I was held as a graduate student by my teachers was, "If you can't illustrate your advice, don't give it." In writing this book, I have had this standard constantly in mind. As a result, this book differs from many others in the literature because it includes detailed examples, from around the world, of how the principles I advocate are manifested in the interpersonal work that is central to leading improvement.

FOUNDATIONAL IDEAS

At the heart of this book is a comparison between two approaches to improvement: the less effective but typical **bypass** approach and the rare but far more effective **engagement** approach.

Whether they are policy makers or network, school, or team leaders, leaders typically use the bypass approach. They lead change by perceiving a problem, designing or selecting a solution, and then leading or delegating its implementation. I call this the bypass approach to change because the leader has not rigorously investigated the beliefs, values, and material conditions that sustain the practices they wish to change. Without such inquiry, change leaders do not know, **from the perspective of implementing agents**, what is involved in making the change they seek. Improvement is driven from a future-focused agenda rather than from a deep understanding of how that agenda is likely to interact with the forces that sustain current practice. Leaders may consult extensively with stakeholders, but unless the focus of such consultation is inquiry into the beliefs, values, and material conditions that sustain the practices they wish to change, they have still employed the bypass approach.

In the engagement approach, leaders inquire into the forces that sustain the practices and outcomes they wish to change. As a result, they gain a deep understanding of the interactions between those practices and their change agenda. This approach is more effective because improvement does not involve the adoption of new practices but their integration into a complex repertoire of existing personal, interpersonal, and organizational practice.

Achieving that integration usually requires eliminating some practices and adjusting others, as well as adopting some that are entirely new.

The collective cognitive and physical effort involved in learning how to do this is motivated by a shared sense of dissatisfaction with the status quo and a determination to reach for something better. Motivating and coordinating this effort is a key leadership challenge. How do leaders communicate their dissatisfaction with the status quo in a way that is uplifting rather than demoralizing? How do they lead the search for something better when they themselves may not know the answers and when others have very different views of what counts as improvement? How do they continually learn with others about whether the proposed alternative practices are likely to deliver the intended improvement?

When it comes to the question of what counts as improvement, the stance I take in this book is that educational improvement is judged by its impact on learners—whether those impacts are social, cultural, or academic. Instead of taking for granted that change will lead to improved outcomes for learners, the history of educational reform tells us that we should do the opposite. In other words, we should assume that change will not deliver our intended improvement unless there are structures and interpersonal processes in place for ensuring that all involved can ensure that change produces the intended improvement.

The structures I describe in this book are the four phases of engagement involving agreeing on the problem to be solved; revealing the tacit theory (beliefs, values, actions, and consequences) that sustains the current practices; evaluating the relative merit of the existing and proposed theories; and implementing and monitoring the new theory of action. Despite the apparent linearity of this four-phase sequence, the engagement approach frequently involves repeated cycles of each phase and considerable overlaps between them.

While the four phases provide a structural guide to the engagement approach to improvement, leaders need, in addition, practical guidance about how to overcome the numerous interpersonal challenges involved. That is why I include within the description of each phase numerous conversation extracts to show precisely what engagement looks like and how it differs from the interpersonal processes typically associated with the bypass approach. These extracts provide clear links between leadership ethics and the interpersonal practices that promote a collaborative, rigorous, and focused approach to improvement.

HOW THIS BOOK IS ORGANIZED

This book progresses through a logical argument about how to reduce change in order to increase improvement. I begin by discussing the importance of distinguishing between change and improvement and of judging educational improvement by its impact on learners (Chapter 1). In Chapter 2, some key concepts that are essential to leading improvement are introduced, including the concepts of theory of action and single- and double-loop learning. Armed with these concepts, readers can then deeply understand the distinction between the bypass and engagement approaches to leading improvement (Chapter 3). The four phases of engagement are elaborated and illustrated in Chapter 4. In Chapters 5 and 6, I discuss the implications of theory engagement for leadership learning. Drawing on a rich data set of real coaching conversations, I analyze the work of one principal coach who was particularly skilled in improving principals' capability by engaging rather than bypassing the values and beliefs that explained their current practice (Chapter 5). Chapter 6 discusses how to design leadership learning in a way that engages rather than bypasses the theories of action of participants. Once again, a real case, involving the design and redesign of a two-day course on principal well-being, is used to contrast the typical bypass design with one that engages the beliefs and values that explain the current practice of participants.

At the end of each chapter, there are Reflection and Action sections that I hope will prompt collaborative reflection on and improvement of the way you lead improvement in your context.

Acknowledgments

This book would not have been possible without my numerous collaborations with system and school leaders around the world. Their challenges have challenged me to think harder and teach better about how to overcome barriers to improvement. Practicing leaders usually have a clear idea about how to lead change, and their ideas provide tough tests of my own.

My work with the Bastow Institute of Educational Leadership in Victoria, Australia, has been seminal in my own learning about leading improvement. My thanks go to Darryl Diment for permission to use his Spelling Story and to Denise Veltre for the Bell Story. Thanks go to Bruce Armstrong, Neil Barker, and Garry Embry for permission to include the case on the design of professional learning (Chapter 6).

A second source of the examples used in this book is the research program my colleagues and I have been pursuing for the last five years on leadership capabilities. Much of the evidence we have collected and analyzed is in the form of transcripts of the real or rehearsed conversations that leaders have held with those involved in their particular improvement efforts. I am grateful to my research colleagues at the University of Auckland—Deidre Le Fevre, Frauke Meyer, and Claire Sinnema—for this research collaboration and to my graduate students—Jacqui Patuawa, Aaron Peeters, and Kelly Slater Brown—for their insights and examples. The team at Vanderbilt University, Tennessee, led by Ellen Goldring, gave me access to their database on coaching without which I could not have developed the material in Chapter 5.

The team at Corwin has been infinitely patient and supportive of this project. My particular thanks go to Arnis Burvikovs, Desirée Bartlett, and Peter DeWitt.

About the Author

Viviane Robinson is a distinguished professor in the faculty of Education and Social Work at the University of Auckland, New Zealand, and academic director of its Centre for Educational Leadership. Her research identifying the impact of different types of leadership on student outcomes (*Student-Centered Leadership*) has been used to shape leadership policy and practice in Scandinavia, England, Singapore, Chile, Canada, Australia, and New Zealand.

She has received numerous awards from national and international professional and academic organizations, including the Australian Council for Educational Leaders, the New Zealand Secondary Principals Association, and the U.S.-based University Council on Educational Administration. In 2011, she was made a fellow of the American Educational Research Association for sustained excellence in educational research. In 2016, the Royal Society of New Zealand awarded her the Mason Durie Medal for her international contributions to educational leadership research and practice. She currently leads a research and development program on the leadership knowledge and skills involved in school improvement.

To learn more, visit her website at www.education.auckland.ac.nz/vmj-robinson.

To my teachers

Chris Argyris (1923–2013)

Donald Schön (1930–1997)

CHAPTER

1

Too Much Change, Not Enough Improvement

This book makes a deliberate distinction between leading improvement and leading change because the conflation of these two concepts contributes to why we have too much change and not enough improvement. The assumption that change is good is entrenched in the discourse of educational reform. Schools that have not changed recently are labeled as coasting or stagnant, and school leaders go to courses to learn how to "lead change." Teachers who do not share their leaders' enthusiasm for a particular change are labeled as "resistant"—as holding up the march of progress. A similar assumption is made about innovation. Parents choose schools that are innovative in their use of technology, and politicians showcase schools that are early adopters of the latest innovation in school architecture or instructional organization.

Change is too often equated with progress and improvement, despite the fact that they are very different. **To lead change is to exercise influence in ways that move a team, organization, or system from one state to another. The second state could be better, worse, or the same as the first. To lead improvement is to exercise influence in ways that leave the team, organization, or system in a better state than before.**

There are a number of reasons why it is critical to interrupt the assumption that change and innovation are necessarily desirable.

NOT ALL CHANGE IS DESIRABLE

The history of school reform is replete with accounts of changes that have not turned out to be improvements. In their book *Learning to Improve*, Bryk, Gomez, Grunow, and LeMahieu (2015) outline how large-scale changes in the United States, including the transformation of hundreds of high schools into smaller schools, turned out not to be the panacea that was hoped. The failure of this reform was attributable to the faulty but powerful belief that such structural change would bring the pedagogical and pastoral changes required to improve the well-being and achievement of high school students.

The New Zealand government responded in the 1990s to the poor math results in the third Trends in International Maths and Science Study (TIMSS) of elementary students with a widely implemented numeracy initiative. Subsequent TIMSS surveys have shown that since its implementation, there has been an increase in students reporting not enjoying math and a further decline in achievement levels (Caygill, 2013; Chamberlain, 2007). Some researchers attribute this to the instructional grouping process that was encouraged by the numeracy initiative. Teachers used the diagnostic tools to group their students on the basis of assessed math ability and then provided the groups with differential opportunities to learn the math curriculum. The unintended consequence was that well-intentioned efforts to "meet student needs" entrenched initial achievement differences (Hunter, 2010). In this example of failed reform, the problem was not faulty implementation but faulty design and the lack of a rigorous, timely, and independent evaluation.

DISTINGUISH BETWEEN CHANGE AND IMPROVEMENT

If we insist on the distinction between change and improvement, there is likely to be more critical and more thoughtful debate, before large-scale implementation, about the merits of proposed reforms.

The Distinction Between Change and Improvement Increases Leaders' Accountability

By making the distinction between change and improvement, we increase leaders' responsibility for developing and communicating the detailed logic of how their proposed change will produce the intended improvement. Too often, leaders ask others to make changes without clearly communicating and debating their arguments for doing so. The New Zealand education system is currently going through the biggest change since the introduction of its radical school self-management reform in 1989. New Zealand's highly autonomous schools are now being encouraged to form loose networks of schools bound together by a common achievement challenge. The intent of the policy is to increase the opportunity for schools to work together, learn from and with each other, and share expertise and good practice. This rationale has been communicated to educators, albeit in a somewhat abstract way. What has

> By making the distinction between change and improvement, we increase leaders' responsibility for developing and communicating the detailed logic of how their proposed change will produce the intended improvement.

not been clearly articulated by policy makers is why they believe that participation in such communities will achieve the overarching educational purpose of the reform, which is to reduce New Zealand's persistent problem of highly inequitable educational outcomes.

The critical question to debate is why, for any given school, participation in a community of schools is more likely to improve the excellence and equity of its students' achievement than the efforts that have been taken to date by the senior leaders of that school. If those senior leaders have been unable to reduce long-standing achievement disparities, despite the initiatives and expertise they have already accessed, then how will their membership in a community make a difference? This question invites a focused debate about the likelihood that the proposed change will be any more successful than the status quo in addressing the central educational problem that the reform is intended to ameliorate. It provides tough tests of the change strategy and helps identify the conditions that are needed if the reform is to deliver the intended improvement.

Such a debate is quite different from a vaguely specified process of "consultation" with relevant stakeholders. The purpose of consultation should be to gain a greater understanding of the conditions required if the change is to produce the intended improvement; the extent to which those conditions are already in place; and, if they are not, how they can be created. The initial consultation will not provide definitive answers, as **collective inquiry is needed throughout the change process in order to learn** what the required conditions might be in different contexts and at different points in time. However, if educators experience their leaders as listening and as responding to feedback in ways that build a more compelling theory of improvement, trust will grow, and they will become more internally and less externally committed to the change. As I write, many New Zealand school leaders are agreeing to form communities of schools because they want access to the professional development money that will be made available to those schools that sign up. How much better it would be if they were signing up because they understood and were fully committed to the educational arguments about why this particular change might bring the desired improvement in student outcomes.

The Distinction Fosters Vigilance About Whether Change Is Working

Once a change is initiated, the distinction between change and improvement encourages more vigilance about how to make the change deliver the intended improvement. No matter how thorough and thoughtful the initial debates about change, there is always considerable uncertainty about what conditions are required to turn change into improvement and about how to create those conditions in different contexts. Good ideas sometimes fail to generate reliable improvement because neither the advocates nor the implementing agents know how to execute them in ways that deliver the intended improvement. As Bryk et al. (2015) write, "We consistently fail to appreciate what it actually takes to make some promising idea work reliably in practice" (p. 6). Instead of taking for granted that change will lead to improvement, we should do the opposite—that is, believe that change will not deliver our intended improvement unless there are structures and processes in place for ensuring that all involved can learn how to turn change into the intended improvement.

> Instead of taking for granted that change will lead to improvement, we should do the opposite—that is, believe that change will not deliver our intended improvement unless there are structures and processes in place for ensuring that all involved can learn how to turn change into the intended improvement.

Is the Change Worth It?

Change is an extremely disruptive and costly process, in both a material and psychological sense. Of course, people resist rather than embrace change, for change takes time, money, and effort. If the implementing agents are teachers, they not only have to learn, for example, how to teach, assess, or relate to students differently, but also how to adjust all of the other practices with which the new ones must articulate. The cognitive and practical effort required to make these adjustments is usually greater than learning the new practices in the first place.

My intention in stressing the distinction between change and improvement is not to somehow defend the status quo or diminish the importance of making large-scale and difficult changes. If we are to make the difference we seek, however, we do need to reduce the number of failed change efforts by being more thoughtful, before changes are adopted, about their likelihood of success and about the conditions required to ensure improvement. Once change is initiated, we need to be humbler about the challenge of implementation and about how much all of those involved have to learn about how to turn the change into the intended improvement. My goal is to help leaders reduce change in order to increase improvement.

IMPROVEMENT MEANS POSITIVE IMPACT ON LEARNERS

Talk of improvement immediately invites difficult questions about what counts as improvement. In this section, I argue that the best indicator of whether or not the changes that leaders make constitute improvement is their impact on learners. This test is consistent with the widely shared moral purpose of education, which, broadly speaking, is to enable all children and young people to succeed at intellectually engaging and enriching tasks and, in so doing, to become confident and connected lifelong learners.

It is one thing for leaders to articulate this moral purpose in policy pronouncements, strategic plans, school assemblies, and team meetings and quite another to use it as a moral compass in day-to-day leadership decisions. Part of the difficulty in using this indicator of improvement is that it is often extremely difficult to tell what course of action is likely to have the greatest positive impact on students. Even if there is relevant research evidence available, that evidence may be conflicting, not accessible to the leader, or not applicable to his or her particular context.

In the absence of widely shared and reliable knowledge about how to make a positive impact on particular social or academic outcomes of learners, other indicators of "what works" have taken the place of evidence about impact on learners. After a recent presentation I gave to Danish school leaders, the director of the local authority (commune) governing the region's schools confessed that he and his staff had assumed that timely completion of project milestones would inevitably be associated with positive impact on students. Timely completion had become the indicator of improvement because it was assumed that correct implementation of the reform guaranteed better student outcomes. Rather than testing the relationship between timely completion and student outcomes, commune leaders had assumed it would be positive.

Another substitute indicator of improvement is change in teachers' practice or attitudes. While teachers' reactions to change are important, the moral purpose of education requires leaders to avoid the assumption that such reactions are reliable correlates of positive impact on students. In a comprehensive systematic review of research on teacher professional learning, Timperley, Wilson, Barrar, and Fung (2007) used impact on the students of the participating teachers as their indicator of improvement. One big finding was how few studies had measured such impact. Measures of teacher satisfaction and of implementation of the professional learning were far more common. A second big message was that correct implementation of the new practices does not guarantee improvement in student outcomes. In a few of the studies included in the systematic review, student outcomes declined when teachers implemented the new practices. This happens when teachers conscientiously implement a change that has not been proven to make the difference that is claimed. This is probably what happened in the New Zealand numeracy project—it was scaled up without sufficiently rigorous and independent evaluations. There was a problem to be solved (disappointing math results) and passionate and articulate advocates of a solution (the numeracy project). What was missing was leadership at the national level that insisted on early engagement with its critics and rigorous independent evaluation of the project's impact on the attitudes and achievement of students.

It is considerably easier now for educational leaders to access the accumulated evidence about the likely impact of any particular change effort on student outcomes than it was twenty or even ten years ago. Rather than rely on a few frequently contradictory studies, leaders can now access systematic reviews (see evidenceforessa.org and ies.ed.gov/ncee/WWC) of the accumulated empirical literature on the likely impact of a proposed reform process on student outcomes. It is important to remember, however, that research findings provide generalizations rather than certainties about the likely impact on students of introducing any particular change. They may help us to select interventions that increase the chances of gaining improvement, but those involved in the change need, in addition, to conduct ongoing inquiries into the impact of the change so everyone can learn how to make it work for students in their own context. Leaders must be willing, at key stages of the change process, to ask, "Is the change likely to or actually delivering improvement?"

THE IMPACT OF LEADERSHIP ON STUDENT OUTCOMES

The pressure has never been greater on school leaders at all levels to improve outcomes for students. The public availability of international comparisons of student achievement across multiple country and state education systems has made policy makers very aware of the consequences of their current policy settings for student outcomes. Overall, underperformance of systems—or of particular social groups within those systems—is receiving unprecedented levels of attention. System-level efforts to improve student outcomes nearly always include assessing and building the capability of school leaders to lead improvement in their own contexts (Mourshed, Chijioke, & Barber, 2010).

Politicians, policy makers, and the public at large are right to focus on the quality of leadership. While such quality is, of course, only one of multiple in-school and out-of-school influences on student achievement, it is the second most important, after teaching quality, in-school influence on student outcomes (Leithwood, Harris, & Hopkins, 2008). Nearly every evaluation of school improvement will partially attribute its degree of success to the quality of leadership (Robinson & Timperley, 2007). Leadership is the enabler of improvement, orchestrating the various conditions, such as professional capability, community engagement, and quality instruction, that need to be working together if improvement in student outcomes is to be achieved and sustained (Bryk et al., 2015).

Given the overall impact of leadership on student outcomes, it is important to ask, "What do leaders need to do to improve outcomes?" and "How do they do it?" Recent research has provided considerable insights into the first question. In the remainder of this section, I briefly review the evidence about *what* leaders of high-performing or improving schools do, so it can serve as a background to the second question about *how* they lead improvement. It is this second question that is the central focus of this book.

In the last fifteen years, new empirically grounded theories of educational leadership have emerged that are based on the educational work of school leaders rather than borrowed from business leadership. Variously called instructional, pedagogical, or educational leadership, these theories are increasingly based on empirical studies of the relationship between particular types of leadership and student outcomes. In my 2011 book *Student-Centered Leadership,* I presented a systematic quantitative review of such studies, called a meta-analysis, and reported the average effects of five dimensions of educational leadership on student outcomes (Robinson, 2011; Robinson, Lloyd, & Rowe, 2008). The dimensions and their average effects on student outcomes are shown in Figure 1.1. The order of the five dimensions is determined not by the size of their effects but by the story they tell of how leaders make a difference to student outcomes.

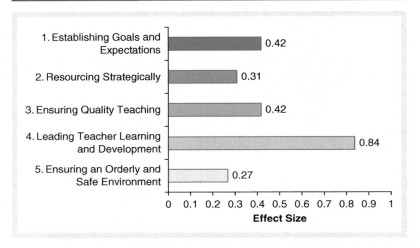

Figure 1.1 Average Effects of Five Dimensions of Educational Leadership on Student Outcomes

Source: Robinson, V. M. J. (2011). *Student-Centered Leadership*. San Francisco, CA: Jossey-Bass, page 9.

In brief, leaders make an impact by setting goals on the basis of the curriculum, community priorities, and evidence about student learning needs (Dimension 1). They then allocate materials, money, and staffing to the pursuit of those goals (Dimension 2). As leaders ensure quality teaching by supporting and evaluating the quality of the curriculum and teaching (Dimension 3), they learn more about what they and their staff need to learn in order to achieve their priority goals. Leaders can then make a considerable impact by leading the teacher learning and development required for goal achievement (Dimension 4). The effects of Dimensions 1 through 4, however, are unlikely to occur without sufficient attention to Dimension 5—creating an orderly and safe environment. As I say to newly appointed principals, if you discover, on taking up your new appointment, that getting teachers and students to class on time is one of your biggest challenges, then start with the practices involved in Dimension 5.

In summary, perhaps the biggest message to come out of this research is that "the more leaders focus their relationships, their work, and their learning on the core business of teaching and learning, the greater their influence on student outcomes" (Robinson et al., 2008, p. 636). So we now have considerable research evidence confirming what the public and the profession knew all along: that leadership matters. But more than the confirmation of common sense, this research has also shown that some types of leadership are much more likely to make a positive difference to students than others.

Since the publication of this work, I have discussed its implications with hundreds of school leaders in many different countries. While the great majority espouses developing stronger student-centered leadership in their school, they struggle with the fact that by becoming "closer to the classroom," they may need to challenge and change long-standing norms and traditions about how leaders interact with their staff. Some leaders talk to me about how strong norms of professional autonomy preclude challenging teaching practice; some high school leaders say they are not confident about their theory of teaching effectiveness and so are reluctant to provide feedback about another's teaching. Team leaders sometimes tell me that they do not feel any responsibility for their colleagues' teaching practice because they have no positional authority over their team members.

> There are many reasons why leaders' change efforts do not lead to improvement, but the reasons I am interested in are those that lie within the control of leaders themselves.

But just as often, leaders recount examples where they have taken responsibility for leading improvement but been unsuccessful in their efforts because teachers have not changed their practice in the intended ways. There are many reasons why leaders' change efforts do not lead to improvement, but the reasons I am interested in are those that lie within the control of leaders themselves. This means focusing on the reasoning and action they bring to the change process. It is there that the keys lie to increasing the chance of making changes that result in improvement. That is why in the rest of the book, I focus on *how* to lead educational improvement.

● ● ● ● REFLECTION AND ACTION

1. In your organization, is a careful distinction made between change and improvement, or is it assumed that changing is equivalent to improving?

2. Discuss how you could interrupt the assumption that changing your system, organization, or team is the same as improving it.

3. How much change is taking place in your context? What do you know about whether it is leading to improved outcomes for learners?

CHAPTER
2

Understand the Challenge of Improvement

Most leaders want to get on with change—their own passion drives their agenda and timetable, sometimes combined with external pressure to improve. They articulate their vision and goals and build coalitions for creating the future they envisage. But change does not happen by focusing only on the future. For change to succeed, leaders need to focus as much, if not more, on understanding the practices they wish to change as on designing the alternatives they seek to introduce. My reason for this claim is that the hardest part of change is not its planning but its implementation because that involves the uncertain and complex process of integrating and aligning the new practices with hundreds of existing practices.

Take the example of a reform strategy designed to improve students' mathematical and scientific problem solving. The strategy requires math and science teachers to use rich texts rather than their current simplified summaries and worksheets; to teach subject-specific literacy practices in addition to the math and science content on which they typically focus; and to lead extended discussions of the material rather than rely on short quizzes and direct instruction. For many high school teachers, adopting such pedagogy requires a shift, not only in their behavior but also in their associated beliefs and values. To the extent that math and science teachers believe that the teaching of literacy is the job of the English department, that they cannot teach subject-specific literacy as well as subject content, and that the use of rich rather than simplified texts will create classroom management problems, they will not adopt the new practices unless forced to do so. These beliefs go to the heart of professional identity ("I'm a science and not an English teacher") and touch on professional capabilities that go well beyond science and math teaching ("How will I control the class if I give them difficult texts?").

UNDERSTAND THEORIES OF ACTION

This example shows that practices that are the target of change are the outward manifestations of a tacit personal theory about how to achieve one's goals—what Argyris and Schön (1974, 1996) call a theory of action (Figure 2.1).

> Practices that are the target of change are the outward manifestations of a tacit personal theory about how to achieve one's goals.

Theories of action have three components: the actions (these are behaviors), the beliefs and values that give rise to those actions, and the intended and unintended consequences of those beliefs and actions (Robinson, 2014b). From the point of view of the observer, a theory of action explains the observed actions by identifying the beliefs and values that sustain them. To return to my previous example, in the left-hand column of Figure 2.2, I have depicted the theory of action of Claudia, a math teacher who exemplifies the beliefs and behaviors of teachers struggling to lift the achievement of their students in math and science problem solving. If Claudia's leader were able to discover

Figure 2.1 The Structure of a Theory of Action

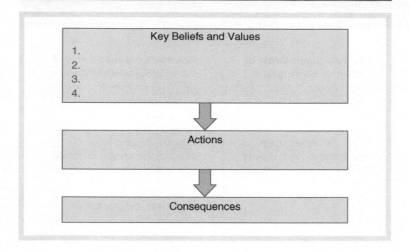

her theory of action, she would then understand the powerful causal linkages between what Claudia does (uses worksheets and simplified texts; uses direct instruction and does not teach math literacy strategies), why she does it (she believes that these teaching strategies enable her to cover the curriculum and control her class), and the consequences of those beliefs and actions (her students have few opportunities to learn comprehension strategies and continue to underachieve despite their teacher having "covered" the curriculum).

In this example, the actions referred to are those of an individual teacher. But since actions occur at individual, group, organizational, and even societal levels, the concept of a theory of action applies to any of these units of analysis (Argyris & Schön, 1996). Appropriate inquiry may show that Claudia's theory of action is common to a number of math teachers, in which case it provides an explanation of the behavior of a team or group of teachers. Similarly, if policy makers were to inquire into the theories of a national sample of high school math and science teachers, they might find that this or similar theories accurately depicted the work of many teachers.

Once we understand the relevant theory of action, we understand what maintains the existing practice and what might be involved

Figure 2.2 A Comparison Between Claudia's Current and Possible Future Theory of Action for Teaching Math

Claudia's current theory of action for teaching math	Her leader's preferred theory of action for Claudia's teaching
Key Beliefs and Values 1. My job is to cover the curriculum 2. It's the job of the English department to teach literacy 3. My students will struggle with more complex texts and misbehave	**Key Beliefs and Values** 1. My job is to teach for understanding 2. Literacy teaching is the job of all teachers and is integrated with teaching of subject content 3. With support, I can learn how to engage students in learning from more complex texts
Current Actions 1. Use simplified texts and worksheets 2. Teach math and science content only 3. Teach through direct instruction of content 4. Assess accuracy of answers	**Proposed Actions** 1. Use rich texts 2. Teach content and subject-specific literacy practices 3. Lead extended discussions of the material 4. Assess oral and written comprehension and problem-solving processes
Actual Consequences 1. Curriculum is covered 2. Class is under control 3. Students score low in problem solving and comprehension	**Future Consequences** 1. Students understand the concepts and can explain their reasoning 2. Students score high in problem-solving and comprehension

in changing it. We see why the difficulty of change is proportional to the degree of tension between the theories of action in current practice and the theories of action required by the proposed new practice.

> The difficulty of change is proportional to the degree of tension between the theories of action in current practice and the theories of action required by the proposed new practice.

Knowledge of existing theories of action enables leaders to predict the likely reaction to their proposed changes. (For example, a leader who accurately understands Claudia's theory of action should be able to predict the points of tension between her theory and the theory he is proposing.) If Claudia interprets the leader's proposal as requiring her to be something she is not (a teacher of English) and as threatening her hard-won gains in classroom management, then passive or active opposition is likely (Figure 2.2). Far from constituting an opportunity for improvement, the leader's change proposal is likely to be interpreted as making her a less effective teacher, no longer able to cover the curriculum or maintain classroom discipline.

The lesson for the leader is not to back away and sacrifice students' learning for the sake of the teacher. Rather, it is to recognize, through early inquiry into the teacher's theory of action, that there is far more at stake for the teacher than first thought. Careful inquiry into teachers' theory of action gives leaders insight into teachers' concerns and hence access to the levers of change. In the case of Claudia, those levers include making the issue of professional identity explicit and designing professional-learning opportunities that build her capability in the required pedagogy *and* in classroom management.

ESPOUSED THEORIES OF ACTION VERSUS THEORIES IN USE

When Argyris and Schön (1974, 1996) wrote about theories of action, they introduced a critical distinction between theories of action that are espoused (talk theories) and theories of action that are in use (walk theories). Both types have the tripartite structure that I have already described—actions, values and beliefs, and intended and unintended consequences (Figure 2.3). Espoused theories are based on reports of what we have done or intend to do. When a leader describes how she intends to run a meeting, she is giving her espoused theory for that meeting. She is describing the actions she intends to take (divide the staff into small discussion groups), the beliefs and values that explain why she is using small groups (to make the meeting more inclusive), and the consequences she wants to obtain (a more democratic staff culture).

While espoused theories are based on reports of what has or will happen, theories in use are inferred from records or observations of what actually happened. If the leader did exactly what she intended, her theory in use matched her espoused theory of how to lead that meeting. On the other hand, if she spent considerable time introducing administrative items and then solicited staff views directly from the whole meeting rather than from small groups, there would be considerable mismatch between her espoused theory and theory in use. If we want to explain this mismatch, we need to discover the beliefs and values that were responsible for the observed actions. Perhaps values such as administrative efficiency or the need to stay in control became, at that particular time, more important than inclusiveness.

Figure 2.3 Two Types of Theories of Action

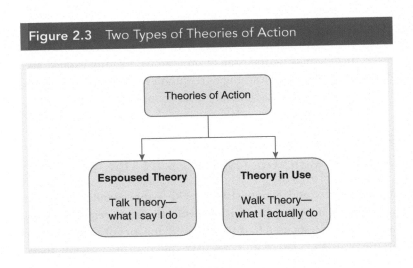

Since we cannot see the beliefs and values that drive our own or others' behavior, it is important to recognize that revealing a theory in use involves making inferences about others' beliefs and values and how they lead to the observed actions and consequences.

Strictly speaking, we are giving *an account of* a person's, team's, or organization's theory in use, and that account may or may not be accurate. In Chapter 4, I give a more detailed description of how we inquire into and check the accuracy of our account of a theory in use.

Espoused theories are important because they express the standards and aspirations against which we want our individual and organizational actions to be judged. A school's vision expresses its important values, its strategic and annual plans communicate how it is going to get there, and its goals and targets express the outcomes it wants to achieve. These are the three components of the school's overarching espoused theory of improvement. If school leaders are strongly committed to their espoused theories, evidence of mismatches between espoused and in-use theories of action should motivate the effort required to reduce the gap.

Reducing the gap involves inquiry into the beliefs and values that drive the discrepant behavior, for they provide important clues about what is involved in reducing it. One of the key lessons to be learned from Argyris and Schön is that since human behavior is anchored in theories in use, the target of change is not actions but the theories in use that sustain them.

> Since human behavior is anchored in theories in use, the target of change is not actions but the theories in use that sustain them.

In many cases, especially when resistance is anticipated, accurately identifying such theories should be part of the design of an improvement strategy. After all, if leaders don't understand the factors that sustain current practice, they don't understand what is involved in improving it.

HELPING TO CHANGE
THEORIES OF ACTION

Inquiry into the theories in use that drive current practice tells leaders a great deal about the depth and likely difficulty of achieving the changes they seek. Imagine that Claudia has a colleague whose students also underachieve in mathematical comprehension and problem solving. Unlike Claudia, however, Justin understands that he needs to teach literacy strategies in order to improve the comprehension and problem solving of his students. He simply needs help with learning how to do so. He presents a very different improvement challenge from Claudia, who also lacks the pedagogical strategies but, in addition, believes it is the role of the English department to teach comprehension strategies. In Justin's case, the instructional changes required for improvement are compatible with his current beliefs and values—in Claudia's case, they are not. To use the language of Argyris and Schön, improvement for Justin's students can be achieved with single-loop learning and change, whereas in Claudia's case, such improvement requires double-loop learning and change (Robinson, 2014a).

The loops to which these concepts apply are portrayed in Figure 2.4. In single-loop learning, mismatches between intended and actual consequences are reduced by trying different actions until there is a sufficient match between the intended and actual consequences. In Justin's case this would involve changing his typical lesson from one in which he provides a demonstration problem and then sets numerous practice examples to one in which he explicitly teaches how to interpret a problem description in terms of its underlying mathematical principles. These pedagogical shifts are compatible with Justin's current beliefs about how to teach math.

In double-loop learning, changes are required to beliefs and values, as well as actions. For Claudia, who does not believe that it is her job to teach the specific comprehension skills involved in mathematical problem solving, the relevant pedagogical shifts are unlikely to be sustained unless those shifts are accompanied by shifts in her beliefs about what it is to be a teacher of mathematics.

Figure 2.4 Single- and Double-Loop Learning

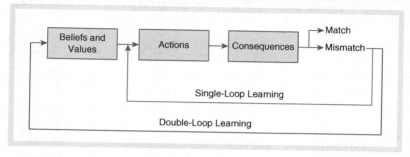

Source: Adapted from Argyris, Chris (1999) (second edition). *On Organizational Learning.* Oxford: Blackwell Business. Figure 3.1, page 68.

The distinction between single- and double-loop learning operates, like the concept of a theory of action, at the level of individual, group, organizational, policy, and even cultural learning.

In a recent professional-learning course I was facilitating, I asked participants to prepare a short presentation for their colleagues on the distinction between single- and double-loop learning and to illustrate their presentation with an original example from their own leadership. Darryl, a middle school principal, declared that his preparation had produced an epiphany: he had finally understood why his attempts to improve spelling in his school had failed, despite this goal being included in the school's strategic and annual implementation plans.

He began his presentation by recounting how, after discussing the spelling data with his staff, the school's leadership team decided to introduce a spelling program called Sound Waves, along with the required resources and staff training. When, after twelve months, the results were no better, they changed to a second program called THRASS and again spent money on resources and staff training. When, once again, the results did not change, a third spelling program called Words Their Way was introduced.

On each occasion, the principal had made single-loop changes because he assumed rather than checked his assumption that his team was as committed to spelling improvement as he was. After all, it was a goal in the strategic and annual plans! If the resources, training, and commitment were present, he reasoned, the lack of improvement must be due to the program itself. The single-loop solution was to change the program. He explained,

> From the beginning, I had assumed that the staff were committed to spelling improvement. However, after facilitating leadership team meetings that began by listening more carefully, it became apparent that some members of the leadership team, as well as some teachers, had quite different beliefs from me about the importance of spelling and that these differences were unresolved. The teachers had been prepared to "give it a go," but some of them felt that it was not as important as reading and writing. They argued that since spellcheck was the way of the future, spelling was now less important.

Improved spelling would not be achieved, regardless of the quality of the program, because teachers were not committed to the goal. The principal stopped the iterative cycles of failed single-loop learning and wasted money and began a more careful discussion about the differing beliefs and values that staff held about the importance of spelling. He shifted from a bypass approach, in which he had unwittingly assumed shared beliefs and values about spelling, to one in which he engaged with others' differing beliefs and thus became open to double-loop learning and change. The outcome was a new commitment to teaching spelling and improved results across the school.

● ● ● ● REFLECTION AND ACTION

1. Involve your team in an exercise to map out their espoused theory for team meetings. Once you have a shared espoused theory, then discuss the match between that espoused theory and the theory that is actually used (theory in use) in your team meetings.

2. If there is a gap between the in-use and espoused theory for team meetings, discuss the causes of the gap, and then make a plan for how that gap can be reduced.

3. Think of a group of students for whom your team has struggled to shift an important academic or social outcome. On reflection, does the distinction between single- and double-loop learning help you explain the difficulty? How can you reduce the temptation to just "try a new approach" when deeper double- rather than single-loop change is needed?

CHAPTER
3

Two Approaches to Leading Improvement: Bypass and Engage

If leaders are to reduce change in order to increase improvement, they need a clear understanding of the difference between the bypass and the engage approaches. The similarities and differences between them are graphically presented in Figure 3.1. In each approach, the leader has a change agenda. Whether that agenda originates with the leader or at another level of the system is immaterial. The point being made is that the team, school, or system leader seeks some type of change.

Moving from left to right in Figure 3.1, we see that change always involves two theories of action: that of the leader and that of the

Figure 3.1 The Bypass and Engage Approaches to Leading Improvement

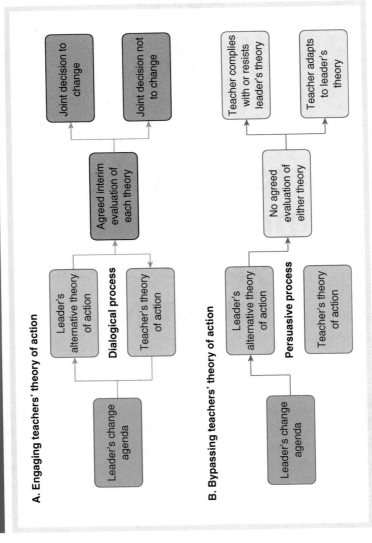

A. Engaging teachers' theory of action

Leader's change agenda

Leader's alternative theory of action

Dialogical process

Teacher's theory of action

Agreed interim evaluation of each theory

Joint decision to change

Joint decision not to change

B. Bypassing teachers' theory of action

Leader's change agenda

Leader's alternative theory of action

Persuasive process

Teacher's theory of action

No agreed evaluation of either theory

Teacher complies with or resists leader's theory

Teacher adapts to leader's theory

Source: Robinson, V. M. J., Hohepa, M., & Lloyd, C. (2009), *School Leadership and Student Outcomes: Best Evidence Synthesis.* Wellington, New Zealand: Ministry of Education.

teachers he or she seeks to influence. The leader's alternative theory is an espoused theory and expresses a vision of how different outcomes could be achieved by teachers if they adopted the leader's agenda. The teachers' theory of action explains and describes what they are currently doing and so is a theory in use.

> In the **engagement approach**, inquiry into the tacit theory that sustains and explains current practice **produces a dialogue** between two theories of action: that of the leaders of the reform and that of the persons they are attempting to influence.

The major difference between the bypass and engage approaches is that in the engagement approach, inquiry into the tacit theory that sustains and explains current practice produces a dialogue between two theories of action: that of the leaders of the reform and that of the persons they are attempting to influence (Figure 3.1). As explained in greater detail in the next chapter, such inquiry involves far more than gaining reactions to or consulting about the leaders' own change agenda. Critically, it also involves deep inquiry into the beliefs and values that drive the current practice and are often the source of objections to the leaders' improvement agenda.

Once the theory in current practice is revealed, its merit can be evaluated in comparison with the proposed alternative. In Figure 3.1, I refer to an agreed **interim** evaluation of each theory as, at the outset of an improvement process, there is considerable uncertainty about whether the leader's proposed change will, if implemented, turn out to be an improvement. In the engagement approach, one outcome of the evaluation is agreement that the current situation is sufficiently unsatisfactory to warrant experimenting with an alternative. Alternatively, the outcome might be agreement that improvement is either not needed or not possible at this time.

In the bypass approach, leaders do not realize—or maybe they ignore—the fact that the actions they wish to change are the visible component of a tacit theory of action. While they may evaluate those actions as less than satisfactory, there is no agreed evaluation of the theory that gives rise to them because the beliefs and values that explain those actions remain invisible.

There are two possible outcomes of this bypass approach. One is adoption of the leader's agenda—a result that recognizes that the bypass approach can produce improvement when it can be achieved with single- rather than double-loop changes (Cohen & Mehta, 2017). After all, teachers can readily adopt and adapt new ideas that fit their current pedagogical repertoire. The other outcome of the bypass approach is that teachers comply with or resist the leader's agenda. Teacher compliance is more likely when they perceive leaders as controlling salient sanctions and rewards. Resistance is more likely when leaders are seen as not having such power.

THE LIMITATIONS OF THE BYPASS APPROACH

While I have acknowledged the conditions under which the bypass approach can be effective, there are a number of important limitations of this approach to leading improvement.

Double-Loop Learning Is Unlikely

When reform ideas are in tension with the values and beliefs of implementing agents—that is, when double-loop change is required—the bypass strategy is unlikely to be effective. This is because the tensions between the existing and alternative theories of action are not resolved, and people are likely to resist making changes they see as incompatible with what they already believe and value. Successful implementation requires identifying and resolving these points of tension, and this is complex and difficult work. In the bypass approach, such work is left to the implementing agents, usually teachers. The result is often a gulf between reform design, implementation, and outcomes, as seen in time delays, stretched budgets, and frustration on the part of both change leaders and implementing agents (Elmore, 2004). Without a detailed understanding of the theories in the practices they seek to change, change leaders will fail to appreciate what their change involves, including the barriers to its implementation.

Too Little Critical Scrutiny of the Alternative Theory

The bypass approach may fail because there is too little critical scrutiny of the alternative theory. The alternative policy, program, or pedagogical practice is presumed by change leaders to be superior to the existing practice. Without critical scrutiny, faulty logic, misalignments between problem causes and proposed solutions, and other flaws in reform design are less likely to be detected than if there is a robust debate about the relative merit of existing and proposed theories of action. Failures of implementation are not the only reason for limited improvement. Poor design of reform programs is an equally important reason (Slavin, 2017).

Bypass May Produce Mutual Mistrust

The bypass strategy can produce mutual mistrust between reform advocates and implementing agents. Implementing agents may not trust reform advocates who have little detailed knowledge of or curiosity about the difference between current practice and their reform agenda. From their point of view, such ignorance means that reform advocates have little idea of the scope and depth of what they are requiring of others. Reform advocates, on the other hand, may not trust the motives of implementing agents, interpreting their objections, slowness, and difficulties as signs of resistance or of being wedded to the status quo. Successful reform requires a strong and sustained coalition between change leaders and implementing agents. Such coalitions build the trust and shared understandings that are critical to a well-coordinated and coherent reform effort (Bryk, Sebring, Allensworth, Luppescu, & Easton, 2010). The bypass approach is unlikely to produce the degree of trust required to forge such a coalition.

> Successful reform requires a strong and sustained coalition between change leaders and implementing agents. . . . The bypass approach is unlikely to produce the degree of trust required to forge such a coalition.

THE BYPASS APPROACH:
A NATIONAL INITIATIVE

Leaders of large-scale reform efforts typically take the bypass approach to educational reform. I stress that this does not mean that they are dictatorial or that they do not consult with stakeholder groups. Rather, it means that they do not systematically inquire at an early stage into the theories of action that sustain and explain the educational practices and outcomes they wish to change. The following story, drawn from a New Zealand national reform effort, illustrates what can happen when reform initiatives are launched without such prior systematic inquiry.

I have already referred to the problem of declining performance and persistent inequity in math achievement in New Zealand. Recent international studies suggest that such inequities are exacerbated by the practice of classroom ability grouping, for such grouping exposes students to very different opportunities to learn mathematics (Schmidt, Burroughs, Zoido, & Houang, 2015). The situation is made even worse by the fact that very few students move out of their initial ability group.

In an effort to address this problem, the New Zealand Ministry of Education launched a math initiative in which lead teachers of mathematics in volunteer elementary schools were trained to teach their students in mixed-ability groups, which functioned as mathematical communities engaged in solving authentic math problems. Once trained, these lead teachers were expected to spread the new approach to the other teachers in their school.

It was this initiative that Kelly, one of my graduate students, chose to study (Slater-Brown, 2016). She asked two simple questions: "Were the lead teachers able to change the instructional grouping practices they used in their own classrooms?" and "Were they, as expected by the initiative, able to change the practices of their colleagues?" Of the six lead teachers she interviewed, all of whom worked in schools serving middle to high socioeconomic communities, one was categorized as making no change in her own classroom practice, two as making little change, and three as making substantial change in their own classroom practice. Given my focus on leadership, it is the second question, about leaders' ability to influence their colleagues' practice, that is of particular interest. Three math lead teachers had no impact on their colleagues' practice, two had a small impact, and only one made a substantial impact.

Through careful interviewing about the theories of action that these lead teachers brought to their leadership role, Kelly discovered some of the reasons for their low impact. These reasons could have been anticipated, debated, and addressed if the designers of the initiative had not bypassed the theories of action of their implementing agents: lead teachers of mathematics and their principals.

The three lead teachers who made no impact did not believe that changing colleagues' teaching practice was part of their role. They each described a strong culture of teacher autonomy in their school and believed it was the responsibility of their principals and other members of the senior management team to challenge and change teachers' instructional preferences. In some cases, they reported attempting to introduce change but had given up, believing that "unless they are a completely united force in the hierarchy of the school that you can't infiltrate and make a difference." In short, these lead teachers believed there was a considerable tension between the role policy makers expected them to play and the culture of their schools.

The critical importance of leadership authority was further suggested by the fact that, unlike the three lead teachers who made no impact, the three who did have some degree of school-wide impact all held deputy principal positions. The one lead teacher who made a substantial impact achieved school-wide change to mixed-ability groups because, in addition to having positional authority, she enjoyed the strong support of her principal, who set the expectation that all staff avoid ability grouping; positioned her as an expert resource; and gave her time to observe teaching, model the alternative grouping and pedagogy, and give feedback to teachers.

As portrayed in Figure 3.1, leaders, who, in this example, were policy makers, may achieve change when using the bypass approach if there is sufficient compatibility between their own theories of action and those of the educators they seek to influence. After all, one of the six lead teachers of math did, with the active support of her principal, achieve substantial reductions in the use of ability grouping in her school. But this was because the conditions that enabled her to be influential with her colleagues already existed (e.g., strong principal support), not because they had been anticipated and planned for by the change designers. The other five leaders achieved little or no change because they either anticipated or encountered resistance from colleagues—resistance that they believed to be legitimized by strong school cultures of teacher autonomy.

My point is that early knowledge of the theories of lead teachers and their principals would have provided a timely warning of the substantial mismatches between the leadership theories of the reform designers (Ministry of Education) and of the implementing agents (principals and their lead teachers). **A change strategy that bypasses the theories in current practice risks ignorance of the conditions that are critical to its success.**

In this example, assumptions about the roles, responsibilities, and capabilities of lead teachers could have been easily tested by short interviews or focus groups at the policy design stage. Questions about what influence they exercise over colleagues, how they exercise it, what the limits of their influence are, and why those limits exist would quickly reveal mismatches between policy makers' and lead teachers' beliefs about how change will occur. Mismatches in beliefs about teacher autonomy over instructional-grouping decisions, the limits of the leadership authority of lead teachers, and the supportiveness of senior leaders could have been identified, debated, and reduced if the improvement strategy had been one of engagement rather than bypass.

FROM BYPASS TO ENGAGEMENT

The process of theory engagement involves revealing the theory or theories in current practice and collaborating with implementing agents in their critique and possible revision. The process is reciprocal in that the change leader's alternative theory must also be explicit and open to revision, especially at those points where there is tension between it and current theories of action. Theory engagement is, in essence, a process of theory competition in which the relative merits of the existing and proposed theories of action are debated (Robinson & Walker, 1999). The result is an agreed interim evaluation of each theory, which, at the outset of the improvement process, might be an agreement not to change or to try something new. In the latter case, the agreement might be based on little more than a shared dissatisfaction with the status quo, which provides sufficient motivation to attempt a change. It would be unreasonable to expect any more commitment from implementing agents before they have experienced the change and seen any evidence of improvement.

> The engagement approach is reciprocal in that the change leader's theory must also be open to revision, especially at those points where there is tension between it and current theories of action.

From Bypass to Engagement: A School Initiative

In contrast to my earlier example about the failure of a national initiative, the following example is about how a principal's initially unsuccessful attempts to improve instructional organization in her own school were transformed when she switched from a bypass to an engagement approach.

The principal wanted to eliminate the ringing of bells every forty minutes during the school day. In her mind, bells were intrusive and, given the amount of lateness to class, were ineffective in promoting punctuality. The solution, as she saw it, was to eliminate bell ringing and have staff and students take more responsibility for being punctual. She promoted her agenda by presenting it to staff and providing reasons why she believed it would be an improvement. In her words, she "did not check whether others agreed there was a problem with punctuality," and when teachers objected, she "did not inquire into their view of the need for bell ringing." Rather, she rebutted their objections and attempted to persuade them by saying such things as, "This is easy; just try it." When she went ahead with the change, the result was staff and student confusion about period times and decreased punctuality. The bells were reintroduced.

The following year, the principal tried again but, this time, engaged rather than bypassed the teachers' views. She began by putting forward her views about how the learning process was disrupted by having a bell ring every forty minutes. In the subsequent discussion, the problem was reframed from a narrow concern about punctuality to a wider concern about how to schedule staff and student time in ways that promoted deep learning. There were still objections to her proposal for a school day that comprised four seventy-five-minute periods instead of seven forty-minute periods, but this time, she listened deeply to her teachers. She learned that they were unsure of how to plan for a productive seventy-five-minute lesson; they doubted that the younger students would stay engaged for seventy-five minutes and that even though this schedule had worked in a neighboring school, they believed their students might be different.

A working party was formed to develop an "Options Paper" and given time to explore how to plan seventy-five minute periods, including visiting similar schools that used such a timetable. Further discussions were held and revised models developed until the teachers' main concerns were alleviated. Teachers began to plan the longer lesson times together, and in the end, there was overwhelming support for and commitment to the new schedule. The result was more teacher cooperation and learning and improved student learning outcomes. As the principal noted, "Punctuality had been a symptom of a school environment where the focus was not on learning and growing." The principal's initial bypass approach set her against her teachers, left her ignorant about the reasons for their objections, and was ineffective in creating improvement. In the subsequent engagement process, a shared, more compelling problem was formulated, and the collective effort of everyone contributed to a solution to which all were committed.

Perhaps the main lesson to be learned from these two examples is that a key initial stage of change leadership is gaining a deep appreciation of the theories that drive the practices you wish to change. I use the word *appreciation* deliberately, for it signals respect and curiosity—attitudes that are critical if change advocates are to learn more about the day-to-day implications of their proposed improvements. For many leaders, this involves a substantial shift in focus from advocacy of their change agenda to collaborative inquiry and evaluation of the relative merits of the current and proposed alternative theories of action. This is what I call leading improvement through theory engagement (Robinson & Timperley, 2013).

● ● ● ● REFLECTION AND ACTION

1. Select the most important reform initiative that you are part of, and discuss the extent to which its leaders are taking a bypass or engage approach.

2. What are the actual and likely consequences of the approach they are taking?

3. What shifts in your collective leadership would increase the chance that this change would produce the intended improvement?

4. Make a plan of action for the changes you have agreed upon.

CHAPTER
4

The Four Phases of Theory Engagement

"Living a satisfying life requires more than simply meeting the demands of those in control. Yet in our offices and class-rooms we have way too much compliance and way too little engagement. The former might get you through the day but only the latter will get you through the night." (Pink, 2009, p. 112)

I n this quote, Daniel Pink captures the contrasting emotional outcomes of leading change in the face of opposition through what I have called a bypass or an engagement approach. In the bypass approach, the goal is compliance, which is achieved by more or less subtle forms of persuasion, bolstered, if necessary, with incentives and various forms of accountability. It leaves the leader winning but at an emotional cost. Engagement, on the other hand, enables you to sleep at night, build trust, and gain the satisfaction of being part of a team that does important work together.

In discussing bypass and engagement with hundreds of leaders, I have not met one who does not want to lead improvement through engaging others' theories of action. Many of them think they already do and are shocked to learn when they listen to their recordings of their leadership conversations that in the face of opposition, their default position is to persuade and bypass rather than to engage.

Leading improvement by engaging theories of action involves four phases: agreeing on the problem to be solved; revealing the relevant theory of action; evaluating the relative merit of the current and alternative theories of action; and implementing a new, sufficiently agreed theory of action (Figure 4.1). In this chapter, I explain and illustrate each phase with extracts of actual or hypothetical conversations between change leaders and implementing agents. These extracts are important, for engagement requires particular interpersonal processes, and an abstract, unillustrated account of each phase would not adequately communicate the interpersonal skills and values involved in these processes.

My frequent contrasts between these engagement processes and the more typical bypass approach further clarify what is and is not involved in leading improvement through engaging others' theories of action. Like all sequential accounts of change, however, the following description greatly oversimplifies its iterative, dynamic, and messy nature (Prochaska, DiClemente, & Norcross, 1992). The arrows in Figure 4.1 represent the iterative processes involved within each phase, as well as the iterative cycle between the four phases.

PHASE I. AGREE ON THE PROBLEM TO BE SOLVED

Why do we need to improve? What is wrong with what we are already doing? What exactly is the problem we are trying to

Figure 4.1 The Four Phases of Theory Engagement

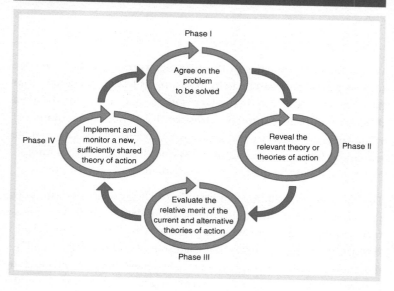

solve? Without compelling answers to these questions, educators will not be committed to the hard work of improvement. Yet many leaders skip this stage of the improvement process, believing that such talk is negative and critical. Instead, they describe their wish to "take advantage of an opportunity" or to adopt something they describe as "best practice." But frequently, such abstract and future-oriented rationales are only weakly motivating, for they fail to answer the inevitable comparative questions, such as why "taking advantage of this opportunity" is better than not taking advantage of it. After all, there are an infinite number of "opportunities for change," and most should probably not be taken. Similarly, appeals to adopt "best practice" imply that current practice is less than best, and such implicit evaluations are more likely to generate mistrust and suspicion than enthusiasm for change.

Shared dissatisfaction with the status quo, coupled with the belief that improvement is possible, motivates the effort required for improvement (Prochaska et al., 1992). Leaders' beliefs about what is problematic and why need to be clearly communicated and rigorously debated in this first phase of the improvement process.

Data Can Suggest What Is Problematic

When describing practice or its outcomes as problematic, reference to trustworthy data can be helpful as long as leaders remember that data do not speak for themselves. Others may interpret the data differently or believe it to be untrustworthy or not representative of what they consider to be important. Nevertheless, data can be extremely helpful in providing powerful checks on the validity of assertions about the quality and consequences of current practice.

The following example, from a study of Data use in United States schools, beautifully illustrates the power of data to challenge educators' assumptions about what is possible with their students (Park, 2008). On hearing the news that their school had been identified by the state as needing improvement, distressed teachers at Lincoln Public School argued that they were doing all that was possible with their students—95 percent of whom were from immigrant backgrounds and qualified for free or reduced price school meals. The standard refrain was that they could not do more, given current resources and the students' behavior and home background.

Administrators challenged the teachers' "we can't do more" attitude by presenting them with data from a school serving students from similar backgrounds, under the same resource constraints, and yet achieving results that put it at the top of the state's rankings. The reaction of teachers was stunned silence. "For once the tendency to blame kids or their families was challenged by the superior student performance of a similar school. For once teachers were forced to consider that children and their families might not be the problem" (Park, 2008, pp. 1–2).

Constructive Problem Talk

Whether or not data are used, leaders' motives in naming something as problematic are critical. An ethos of continual improvement rather than of blaming is needed, and the way to establish such a culture is through what I call constructive problem talk. This involves describing what is perceived to be problematic and the grounds on which that judgment is based, and doing so in a way that invites rather than shuts down any differing views.

> An ethos of continual improvement rather than of blaming is needed. . . . This involves describing what is perceived to be problematic and the grounds on which that judgment is based, and doing so in a way that **invites** rather than shuts down any **differing views**.

Here is an example of what I mean. In the conversation extract in Table 4.1, the principal (Justin) is meeting with a somewhat wary head of English (David) to discuss the latter's written analysis of the national exam results for his students. The process for doing the analysis in a standard template was agreed upon at a prior meeting of the heads of all subject departments.

In this extract, Justin builds trust by repeatedly checking rather than assuming the accuracy of his attributions about David and by disclosing his own evaluation of the results as disappointing. His careful perspectival language ("my reading") creates space for difference and disagreement, and that, combined with his careful checking and empathy, creates a safe space for David to disclose his own disappointment.

> Leaders who engage in constructive problem talk position themselves as part of the problem, as well as part of the solution.

The agreed problem, at this early stage, is that the English results are disappointing. There is a long way to go; agreeing that there is a problem provides no guarantee of agreement about its causes and possible solutions. But sufficient common ground has been established, through honest and nonblaming evaluation, to motivate the next step at least.

Leaders who engage in constructive problem talk position themselves as part of the problem, as well as part of the solution. They reflect on and communicate honestly about their own possible

Table 4.1 Constructive Problem Talk

Speaker	Conversation	Analysis
Justin (principal)	And thank you for giving the template to me in advance because it did give me a chance to read it and to think about what you as head of English had made of these data. And I acknowledge this is the first time we've done this exercise and it's . . .	Justin thanks David and acknowledges the novelty of the task.
David (head of English)	Yes.	
Justin	You know, it's not easy. I mean, you didn't find it easy?	Justin checks his assumption that the task is a complex one.
David	No, no, it was quite a challenging document to fill out, but, anyhow, that's the best I could do in the time I had.	
Justin	Yeah, and as I read it, you're saying that these are weaker results than you would like, certainly that was my reading of those data as well. I mean we've got a few "achieved" grades, but the percentages are disappointing compared to the, some of the other departments and to the benchmark that we talked about using in the heads of . . .	Justin uses perspectival language to create space for a differing view: "and as I read it . . ." " . . . my reading of the data." Justin discloses his disappointment in the results.
David	Yeah, the results are overall, I admit, they're disappointing, and we would like to talk to you about that, yeah, okay, so I agree with you that the achievement is disappointing with some of those kids, yeah, and not unexpected in many ways.	David discloses his disappointment in the results. Both parties agree the results are disappointing. " . . . so I agree with you . . ."

contributions to the problem, whether they are ineffective policies, inadequate resourcing and capability building, or avoidance of tackling a tough issue. In my view, problems that have emerged and persisted during the tenure of a particular leader or leadership team are, by definition, partly the responsibility of that leader or leadership team. This does not mean they are incompetent or should blame themselves or be blamed. It does mean, however, that in naming and inquiring into the problem, they should reflect on and communicate their own, as well as others', potential contributions to the problem. Such acknowledgment begins to build the trust needed to tackle it together.

Defensive Problem Talk

Both avoidance of problem talk and blaming problem talk are ineffective. Our own research evidence suggests that these patterns are much more common than constructive problem talk. In one of our studies (Sinnema, Le Fevre, Robinson, & Pope, 2013), we asked educational leaders to complete a questionnaire about a concern they had about the behavior or performance of someone in their area of responsibility. They described the duration of their perceived problem, the effectiveness of their prior attempts to resolve it, and their own possible contribution to the situation. In 22 percent of cases, the problems these leaders nominated had persisted for between one and two years, and in 12 percent of cases, they had persisted for more than two years. On average, educational leaders rated their prior attempts as minimally effective and the conversations they had as somewhat difficult.

So how did these leaders actually communicate the concerns they had written about? We were able to compare the private descriptions they gave us on their questionnaires with what they said to the person involved because we had both parties' permission to record and transcribe their conversation. For most leaders, there was a considerable difference between how they communicated their concern to the person involved and how they had described it in their questionnaire. In all cases where there was a difference, the concern was described as much more serious, certain, and problematic in the private than in the public context. The following example (Sinnema et al., 2013) is typical in showing how the concern was described more strongly in the private questionnaire than in the public conversation context:

Private context: "A new leader, never been principal before who has been in the job for a few weeks has gone in, mentioned his previous site many times, is not listening to the staff, making changes . . ."

Public context: "We spoke about how important it is to come into the new site and just listen and take time to get to know people and just observe. So how is that going?"

In the public context, the superintendent's concern is moderated, since his focus is on what he wants the newly appointed principal to do (taking time to listen when new to a school) rather than on what he considers to be problematic (the number of times the principal has referred to his previous school). Rather than a clear and open-minded statement of his concern, as is required for constructive problem talk, the superintendent has communicated his concern indirectly through a loaded question. The question is loaded because it presupposes (a) that the principal recalls the conversation (and he may not) and (b) that the principal has followed the superintendent's advice (and he may not have). The question is also controlling because it implies that the principal ought to have done those two things and therefore ought to be able to report on his progress in listening and getting to know people.

It is important to note at this point that the private description, with its greater certainty and stronger negative evaluation, does not meet the standard for constructive problem talk either because it presumes rather than checks the validity of the perceived problem.

Our research on leaders' conversations helps explain why many leaders' problems persist for so long. First, the indirectness of their communication, as seen in generalized statements ("We all have trouble meeting deadlines at times") and loaded questions ("How are you doing with the report deadlines?"), means that the messages are unclear and delivered in a way that signals risk, ambivalence, and the need for diplomacy.

Second, leaders' presumption of the validity of their perception that a situation is problematic reduces trust because it communicates a prejudgment rather than a willingness to discuss the validity of their perception.

Gain Sufficient Agreement

So far, I have discussed how leaders can motivate improvement by disclosing and checking their view that the current situation is less than satisfactory. But we can all think of situations where constructive problem talk fails to recruit staff to the problem-solving process. Sometimes, agreement that the current situation is problematic can still be reached, not by agreeing whether the status quo is good, bad, or indifferent but by agreeing that, whichever it is, it could still be improved. A problem is defined as a gap between a current and desired state of affairs, and people can agree to reduce the gap whether or not they agree on how large it is.

While the initial common ground between the parties might be small, the goal at this early stage is to gain sufficient agreement to begin a collaborative process of improvement. There are situations, of course, where, despite respectful and constructive problem talk, leaders fail to gain sufficient agreement to start an improvement process. In such situations, the leadership must consider whether their duty of care to students requires them to go ahead in bypass mode, being as transparent as they can about what they are doing and why, so that a switch to engagement mode is possible at a later date.

PHASE II. INQUIRE INTO THE RELEVANT THEORY OF ACTION

The purpose of this phase is to create an accurate account of the theory that explains what has been agreed to be problematic. In this section, I describe and illustrate the inquiry processes that enable leaders to achieve this quickly and effectively. Leaders may notice actions or inactions but not know the beliefs that produce them. Conversely, they may see consequences but not know the actions and beliefs that produced them. The goal of their inquiry is to discover all three components and link them together into a logical and accurate account of the relevant theory of action.

In inquiring into theories of action, leaders should keep three main questions in mind. One question is, "What was done or not done?" This question prompts leaders to get information about the action component of a theory in use. The second guiding question—"Why was that done or not done?"—prompts leaders to discover the beliefs and values that explain the actions and inactions. The third question—"What happened as a result?"—prompts leaders to probe for the consequences of the beliefs and actions. The result of successful inquiry into a theory of action is a coherent and accurate account of the links between what was done or not done, why, and with what consequences.

> **Three Guiding Questions for Leaders Inquiring Into Theories of Action**
>
> *What* was done or not done?
>
> *Why* was that done or not done?
>
> *What* happened as a result?

Ask Direct and Respectful Questions

It is frequently assumed by leaders that they don't have time for this type of inquiry. In a sense they are right, for what inquiry they do make is frequently so general and indirect that they waste time skirting around the issues they are really interested in. The reason for their indirectness, they tell me, is that they fear that a more direct approach will strain their relationship. It is my intention in the examples in this section to discuss and illustrate how to inquire into a theory of action in a way that is respectful *and* direct.

In Table 4.2, I continue my analysis of the conversation, first presented in Table 4.1, between Justin, the high school principal, and David, the head of English. Having agreed on the problem

Table 4.2 Direct and Respectful Inquiry Into a Theory of Action

Speaker	Conversation	Analysis
Justin (principal)	Right, so let me just check. One of the reasons why you haven't made suggestions for changing the program is because there's a sort of pattern here that's not surprising you about the way these students are performing.	Justin checks the accuracy of his understanding of David's reasons.
David (head of English)	That's right.	David confirms accuracy.
Justin	Okay. Tell me more about that, David, because it's really important for me to understand your explanation for this pattern of results.	Justin asks David to elaborate on his beliefs and gives a reason for his question.
David	Okay, well, one of the big challenges for us is that getting the students up to standard for [the national examination] is we have three years in total, but you're looking at points of achievement here where not all of those kids were in this school for three years. As you know, we've got a lot of transient kids that come into the school, and the backgrounds of the students coming in, Justin, is just, it's a real problem for us that they're coming into the school either from other schools with very disappointing achievement, and also, our Year 9 intake for that group was really weak in terms of their literacy. And so, we're not surprised that this is the outcome a little further down the track. So disappointment at the level of achievement of the students coming into the school.	David responds with deeper explanation for why he is not surprised at the disappointing results.

(Continued)

Table 4.2 (Continued)

Speaker	Conversation	Analysis
Justin	Okay. So you're saying that you've got a cohort of students this year that may be particularly weak, you're saying that the transience of the students is a problem, and you're also saying that the prior literacy levels of the students coming from the contributing schools is also a problem. Have I got that right?	Justin summarizes and checks.
David	Yes, to all of those things, yeah definitely. And the staff overall feel quite overwhelmed by the extent of this problem that's coming into the school, and it's getting worse, and I mean, you said this cohort, but I know that when I look at Year 10, if I look back a year, that similar concerns are there.	David confirms that Justin has been listening and then goes deeper into how he and his team are feeling.

(disappointing English results), Justin asks why David has not completed the section in the template that solicits information about changes to the teaching program that might address the disappointing results. The reason, David explains, is that he only had time to consult one of his teachers and that "we were not surprised with the pattern of results." The extract begins with Justin checking his understanding of David's reasons.

The action—or more accurately, inaction—that Justin was seeking to explain was David's limited written reflection on how to improve the results in his department. What he learned, in the space of less than a minute, was that David had had limited time to consult with his teachers and that his team attributed the "unsurprising" results to external factors, including poor prior achievement, transience, and home background. Perhaps most important of all, Justin learned that the English department felt overwhelmed by the problem and anticipated similar results from the next year's cohort. Without intervention, the department's theory of action would probably produce similarly disappointing results the following year.

Postpone Evaluation of the Theory

On reading this conversation, some school leaders express strong criticism of the principal for what they see as his acceptance of David's **deficit thinking**. Such criticism reflects a misunderstanding of the purpose of this phase of the engagement approach, which is to **reveal** the relevant theory of action, regardless of its merit. That requires careful listening, summarizing, and checking our understanding of others, regardless of our degree of agreement with their beliefs and actions. In this extract, Justin's nonjudgmental interpersonal behavior enabled David to feel safe enough to take considerable risks—disclosing his beliefs about the external causes of the results and the emotional state of his team. **To listen to and acknowledge a theory of action does not signal agreement with it.** After all, Justin has a duty to lead an improvement process and, unless he is new to the position, to acknowledge his part in the problem and his desire to be part of the solution. The evaluation of David's theory and of Justin's proposed alternative is discussed and illustrated in the next phase of the engagement approach.

Inquire Systematically Into Each Component of the Theory of Action

In the next example, I illustrate how a deep understanding of the three components of a theory of action enables a leader to systematically gather information about each component without marching the other person through an artificial and unresponsive set of questions (see Table 4.3).

The context is that of a senior leader (Dylan) in a high school talking with a middle leader (John) who has asked for help with one of his teachers (Pam) whom he considers to be underperforming. John describes Pamela's students as "not engaged" and "suffering death by PowerPoint." The senior leader (Dylan) believes his role is to build the capability of middle leaders to resolve such issues with their teachers rather than take over and handle them himself. In this conversation, he wants to find out the theory of action that John is using with Pamela.

In less than three minutes, Dylan has revealed the theory of action that explains *how* John is attempting to help one of his teachers, *why* he is taking that approach, and *what the consequences* of his approach are likely to be (Figure 4.2).

By revealing and checking John's theory of action, Dylan has obtained powerful clues about the path to improvement. In this example, improvement would involve increasing John's ability to save time, address his concern, and build trust by having respectful conversations in which he discloses his concern without prejudging its validity. This would involve, among other things, teaching John how to inquire into Pam's theory in use, just as Dylan inquired into that of John. John and Pam could then discuss the links between her teaching beliefs and strategies and the disengagement of her students.

The concept of a theory of action enables us to understand "resistance to change" in a different and hopefully more productive

Table 4.3 Systematic and Responsive Inquiry Into a Theory of Action

Speaker	Conversation	Analysis
Dylan (senior leader)	OK. So with that concern, what have you been able to do about it so far?	Dylan seeks information about John's *actions* to date.
John (middle leader)	We've been focusing in departmental meetings on strategies for cooperative learning and opportunities we can use for group work that can help her, but I haven't targeted her specifically; I've done it for the whole department.	Dylan learns that John's actions have not focused on Pam.
Dylan	Right. So in terms of talking with Pam or anything directly or indirectly helping Pam with this, any other actions you were able to take?	This question checks for any other *actions* taken by John.
John	Umm, nothing really specific.	
Dylan	How effective do you believe the actions you've been able to take so far have been with Pam?	In seeking John's opinion about perceived effectiveness, Dylan is now collecting information about possible *consequences of the actions and inactions*.
John	I think I've sown some seeds.	
Dylan	OK, right. And how effective do you think it's been?	Dylan is not sure of John's answer about effectiveness, so he *repeats the question about consequences*.
John	I think we've got more work to do to develop, change practice. I need to follow that up.	John sees his efforts so far as less than effective.

(Continued)

Table 4.3 (Continued)

Speaker	Conversation	Analysis
Dylan	And how might you do that, if you do intend? (I mean, I don't want to put words in your mouth. Sometimes, you can only do so much . . .)	Dylan seeks information about the *planned future actions* (follow-up).
John	How might I do that? Umm, I'm trying to think of an opportunity to talk to her. I'm not the person who actually does her evaluation, but perhaps I need to talk to the person who does do her evaluation and raise that, but I have been thinking about doing some more walk-throughs to all the department members, and as a result of that, I could give some more specific feedback to teachers I saw, and that could be the starter for a conversation.	John considers (a) talking to Pam's evaluator and (b) doing walk-throughs for all of his staff. These would provide a context for giving Pam feedback.
Dylan	So John, as I listen to you, I'm thinking that in your view, it's not appropriate to do something specifically with Pam. I'm hearing two strategies . . . one is the departmental meeting on cooperative learning and the other is the walk-throughs. Those strategies have been generally targeted—is that a correct summary?	In this summary, Dylan checks his perception of John's *preferred action strategies* (those that provide professional-learning opportunities to all of his staff rather than to Pam in particular).
John	I think it is. If I had more time, I'd love to do more.	John confirms the accuracy of Dylan's summary of his action strategies.

Speaker	Conversation	Analysis
Dylan	You mean do more with . . . ?	Dylan seeks greater specificity about *future actions*.
John	One on one.	
Dylan	So you would like to work one on one?	
John	Yes, but with teaching four classes and trying to cope with all the other administration . . .	This *belief* (time shortage) provides a possible explanation for the lack of one-to-one discussion with his teachers.
Dylan	Right, so one reason why that hasn't happened is time. Are there any other reasons, in your view, why you haven't talked one on one with Pam?	This question *checks for other beliefs that might explain* John's approach to helping Pam.
John	Umm, it's not easy sometimes to have those conversations. You like to keep collegial feeling in the department; we like to keep supportive of each other, but those conversations can be quite difficult.	John *provides a second possible explanation* for his actions and inactions.
Dylan	And what do you sense might be difficult about it?	Dylan *probes John's belief* about the difficulty of working one on one with Pam.
John	Knocking her confidence. I think she already lacks confidence in the class; that's why we have this situation in the first place. So I think that's why—I want to build her up rather than have her think that maybe I'm criticizing her.	Dylan learns that John's belief that he might knock Pam's confidence provides a second explanation of why he has not talked directly with her.
Dylan	OK.	

Figure 4.2 John's Theory of Action for Helping Pam

Key beliefs and values

Pam may learn from general professional discussions

and

Singling out Pam will damage professional relationships

Actions

Lead professional-learning meetings

and

Avoid one-to-one discussions with Pam

Consequences

Pam's teaching is not improving

Her students continue to be disengaged

John is still unable to address issues of teaching quality
with his team

way (Zimmerman, 2006). People resist change when they sense it will conflict with what is important to them, and what is important is signaled in the beliefs component of their theory of action. Those beliefs are the source of objections to any proposed change, and so, if leaders engage with those beliefs, they learn the reasons why people are reluctant to make the changes they propose. Resistance is now understood not as personal opposition to the leader but as a rational response to a perceived threat to what is held dear. Rather than label others as resistant, it is more productive to reframe resistance as theory competition—a reframing that is true to the spirit of theory engagement and invites an explicit process of theory evaluation. It is to that process that I now turn.

PHASE III. EVALUATE THE RELATIVE MERIT OF THE CURRENT AND ALTERNATIVE THEORIES OF ACTION

My frequent references to alternative theories of action may give the misleading impression that I expect leaders to have formulated or accessed full-fledged alternative theories of action early in the improvement process. Such an expectation is reasonable when the intent is to adopt a standardized reform program. In such instances, the engagement approach involves agreeing on the problem, revealing the theory of action in the current practices, and then using agreed-upon evaluation criteria to decide whether to change and, if so, which program to adopt.

Such an expectation is less reasonable in situations where leaders are expected to construct their own strategies for improving site-specific problems of teaching and learning. In those situations, the alternative theory is not well formed at the outset; rather, leaders and implementing agents inch their way toward it through collaborative inquiry and repeated critical evaluation of alternative possibilities.

Leading improvement is a highly evaluative endeavor. In the first phase, reaching agreement about whether the current situation constitutes a problem is explicitly evaluative. Although evaluation is largely set aside in the second phase, it comes to the fore again in this third phase as the parties discuss whether it is worth trying to change the current theories of action.

I frequently hear leaders deny their evaluative role. "I'm not being evaluative," they claim, as they begin a series of classroom observations. But such claims are naïve, for the choices they make about what to observe are based on a theory about what should and should not be happening in the type of lesson they are observing. Their theory tells them how to select what is important from the infinite number of things they could be observing in that class-room. When leaders say, "I'm not being evaluative," what they usually mean is, "I'm not being judgmental," and it is this distinc-tion between being judgmental and evaluative that is important for this phase of theory engagement.

To be judgmental is to presume the validity of one's evaluations and be closed- rather than open-minded about the differing eval-uations of others (Spiegel, 2012). A judgmental leader bypasses rather than engages another's theory and the differing evalua-tions it generates and so precludes the debate and dialogue required to check the merit of the current and alternative theories of action. A nonjudgmental leader of improvement acknowledges the necessity of evaluation, is transparent about his or her pre-ferred evaluative criteria, and is open to others' views about their appropriateness.

Which Values Are Important?

The most common question I encounter about this phase of theory engagement is, "What if we don't value the same things?" The worry is that people may evaluate alternative theories of action very differently because they do not agree on the criteria against which the competing theories are evaluated. For example, in discussing how to improve literacy levels in a particular high school, some teachers give great importance to improving boys' love of reading. Others may be more concerned with fostering what they call deep learning and critical thinking. These differing values mean that teachers will eval-uate alternative literacy programs, including the current one, very differently. Teachers who value deep learning and critical thinking are likely to reject a fast-paced and highly structured program, even though it has good evidence of increasing vocabulary and compre-hension, because they will see it as incompatible with fostering deep learning. Other teachers in the school may reject a program that they believe gives insufficient attention to boys' love of literacy.

The problem here is not that the teachers can't agree on the best literacy program. Rather, it is that they are trying to make that decision without prior agreement on the criteria to be used in the evaluation of the alternative programs. The danger is that people will argue about the best decision to make and then resolve their conflict with some type of compromise, without ever discussing and agreeing on their evaluative criteria. So in the face of such difference, how do leaders lead a discussion that results in an agreed-upon set of criteria? While there is no easy answer to this question, there are helpful guidelines.

Steps for Agreeing Upon a Set of Evaluation Criteria

1. Distinguish between evaluations and evaluation criteria

   First—and perhaps most important of all—keep discussion about the criteria to be used in the evaluation separate from the actual evaluation, and insist that an initial working set of criteria is established first. If this is not followed, then a partisan discussion is likely to ensue in which everyone's preferred but unexamined criteria produce widely discrepant evaluations.

2. Make evaluation criteria explicit

   Second, make all of the proposed criteria explicit. In my brief discussion of the prior literacy example, at least three criteria were implicit in the evaluations reached. An effective literacy strategy was one which improved boys' love of reading, improved comprehension, and fostered critical thinking. Improvement strategies should be evaluated against multiple indicators rather than a single one. This is because success in any particular educational endeavor typically requires doing multiple tasks well. At this stage, teachers are saying they want a strategy that motivates the boys and explicitly teaches comprehension skills and critical thinking. Careful listening to teachers, as well as professional reading, might throw up additional criteria, including practical ones like being within budget, aligning literacy teaching to required assessments, and gaining board approval.

3. Verify whether the criteria are aligned with the analysis of the problem

   Third, reflect on the alignment between the criteria and the analysis of the problem. Improvement will only come if the adopted strategy is well matched to the problem, and a great deal has been learned about that problem by revealing the theory in the current practice. The beliefs, actions, and inactions that are causally implicated in the problem should shape some of the evaluation criteria. For example, if boys' low reading comprehension and negative attitude toward reading are causally linked to the type of texts they are being asked to read, then provision of texts that are attractive to boys should be an important evaluation criterion. If critical thinking is weak because current teaching is fostering recall of factual material, then the improvement strategy needs to give considerable emphasis to teaching comprehension and critical thinking. In short, strong alignment is needed between the analysis of the problem and the criteria that will be used to evaluate the solution alternatives.

4. Examine and understand the relationships between the multiple criteria

   Fourth, once multiple criteria are nominated, discussion can move to understanding them more specifically and examining the relationships between them. What do those teachers actually mean by critical thinking? Do we have a shared understanding of the term so we can agree on how to evaluate the alternative literacy strategies? If we do, how does critical thinking relate to the teaching of comprehension? Is it possible that a certain level of comprehension is a prerequisite for critical thinking?

5. Identify any features of current practice that must be included in the evaluation criteria

   Fifth, ensure that required features of current practice with which any new practice must be aligned and integrated are included in the evaluation criteria. If the district requires certain literacy assessments, then compatibility of the new strategy with those assessments should be an additional evaluation criterion. By paying attention at this early stage to the integration of current and new practice, leaders communicate respect for the complexity of implementation and take responsibility for some of the challenges involved.

Once a working set of evaluation criteria is agreed on, then the criteria can be used to evaluate alternative theories of literacy improvement, including the theory in current practice. When a new literacy strategy is being selected from a range of standardized alternatives, the question is, "How well do each of the alternatives satisfy our various criteria?" Of course, none will satisfy them all, and there will not be time to research all of the possibilities, but at least a systematic and transparent process ensues in which everyone is aware of the trade-offs and the reasons for the eventual decision.

When an alternative strategy is being constructed rather than selected, the question is, "How do we design a literacy strategy that, as far as possible, satisfies our various evaluative criteria?" The task here is a very creative one, drawing on and developing expertise in teaching critical thinking and comprehension so a program eventuates that has a high likelihood of increasing student outcomes in both these areas, while increasing boys' love of reading and doing so without blowing the budget.

Theory Evaluation and Interpersonal Behavior

The evaluation phase of theory engagement presents interpersonal challenges, particularly if critical feedback is involved. This is especially true if the theory of action being evaluated is that of only one or two individuals, for people can feel singled out and unfairly treated. Leaders usually describe these interpersonal challenges as a tension between communicating their honest evaluation and maintaining their relationship with the recipient of their feedback. In ten years of research on this challenge, my colleagues and I have learned quite a bit about its origins and how it can be overcome.

One of the main data sources we use in this research is transcripts of leaders' conversations with a colleague. The purpose of these conversations is to communicate and discuss a real concern that the leader has about an aspect of the behavior or performance of a colleague. Despite the explicitly evaluative purpose of these conversations, we were surprised to find very little explicitly evaluative talk. We knew from the questionnaires completed prior to the conversations and from probing leaders' unexpressed thoughts that the absence of such talk was not due to them being uncertain about their evaluation. Rather, it was a reluctance to communicate it directly to the person involved.

The bottom left-hand side of Figure 4.3 illustrates leaders' typical "withhold evaluation" strategy. Rather than disclose their own evaluation, they ask the other person to disclose theirs, in the hope that it will be similar to their own. Even though this strategy involves inquiry into the other's views, it is not engagement because **engagement requires both parties to have access to each other's thinking.** In this example, the criteria the leader used to judge the reading program and the resulting evaluation have been kept secret.

In our research data, the second "judgmental" strategy is far less common. Leaders tend to resort to it when they are under pressure from administrators or parents. The words are judgmental,

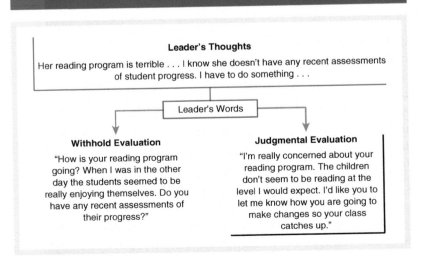

Figure 4.3 Two Forms of Bypass in the Communication of Critical Evaluations

Leader's Thoughts

Her reading program is terrible . . . I know she doesn't have any recent assessments of student progress. I have to do something . . .

Leader's Words

Withhold Evaluation

"How is your reading program going? When I was in the other day the students seemed to be really enjoying themselves. Do you have any recent assessments of their progress?"

Judgmental Evaluation

"I'm really concerned about your reading program. The children don't seem to be reading at the level I would expect. I'd like you to let me know how you are going to make changes so your class catches up."

for they assume the appropriateness of the leader's evaluation criteria and of the evaluation itself. The leader bypasses the thinking of the teacher in a classic "I'm right; you are wrong" move.

When we asked leaders about the mismatch between their highly evaluative thoughts and their generally nonevaluative talk, we learned that they withheld their evaluations for fear of upsetting or damaging their relationship with their colleague. We now understood why they felt caught between being honest and preserving their relationship. Their thoughts were so definitive and certain that they left no room for a differing point of view. It certainly would be upsetting, if not downright rude, to communicate them. The key to avoiding the dilemma is not to tone down or withhold the words but to change the thinking that produces such a judgmental evaluation.

> The key to avoiding the dilemma is not to tone down or withhold the words but to change the thinking that produces such a judgmental evaluation.

When leaders frame their critical evaluations as definitive and certain, engagement becomes irrelevant because they are convinced they are right. The other person becomes an object for persuasion to one's own point of view, and the dilemma is how to do that without too much upset. Whether the avoidance or judgmental strategy is used, each is disrespectful. Respect requires elimination of the certainty and judgmental language, together with genuine interest in the other's evaluative stance. This reframing enables both parties to share and discuss their evaluations of the reading program. In Figure 4.4, the leader reframes her thinking from the definitive judgment that "the program is terrible" to the more perspectival and specific, "I think the children are well behind." In addition, she shifts from the closed-minded stance, suggested by, "I have to do something" based on my correct judgment, to the more open-minded determination to check how her own evaluation compares with that of the teacher. The reframing produces a much closer match between the leader's thoughts and words. The leader has been honest about her evaluation

Figure 4.4 From Bypass to Engage in the Communication of Critical Evaluations

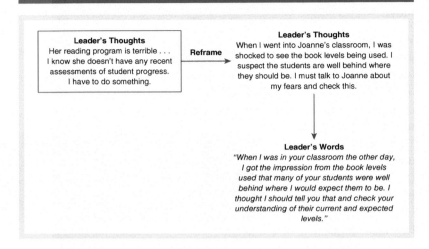

Leader's Thoughts
Her reading program is terrible . . . I know she doesn't have any recent assessments of student progress. I have to do something.

Reframe

Leader's Thoughts
When I went into Joanne's classroom, I was shocked to see the book levels being used. I suspect the students are well behind where they should be. I must talk to Joanne about my fears and check this.

Leader's Words
"When I was in your classroom the other day, I got the impression from the book levels used that many of your students were well behind where I would expect them to be. I thought I should tell you that and check your understanding of their current and expected levels."

yet done so in a way that invites the other's point of view and makes room for difference. There is now no dilemma between being honest and respectful.

Communicating Respectful Evaluations

In my ideal organization, critical evaluation would be an accepted part of a professional-learning culture. It would be communicated in everyday professional conversations and not confined to formal teacher evaluation or performance review contexts. Leaders and teachers would provide and seek critical feedback and be highly skilled at formulating their critique in ways that enabled them to express it spontaneously, honestly, and respectfully. Such skills are crucial if teachers are to learn from one another in professional-learning communities and networks. Given the paucity of such critical talk (City, Elmore, Fiarman, & Teitel, 2009), I conclude this section on the third phase of engagement with an illustrative example of one such conversation.

In the extract (Table 4.4), I return to the conversation between Justin, the high school principal, and David, his head of English.

In prior discussion of this conversation, we saw how David explained the disappointing student results in term of factors that lay outside his classroom: prior achievement, home background, and student mobility. Justin then carefully checked his understanding of David's explanation before offering an alternative view.

Table 4.4   Direct and Respectful Evaluation of a Theory of Action

Speaker	Conversation	Analysis
Justin (principal)	Yeah, okay. Well, David, I think it would be really inappropriate of me to rule out any of those explanations of this pattern of achievement because, quite frankly, we as a school are just starting on this journey of using the evidence to test and check our explanations. The common ground that we've got is neither of us is happy with the pattern of achievement.	Justin remains open to David's explanations, as their validity has not yet been checked. He reiterates the previously established common ground: shared dissatisfaction.
David (head of English)	No.	
Justin	You and I are concerned about your teachers working to introduce new innovations and new approaches that are not working well enough, and I actually am pleased that we're having this conversation and that we can start doing something to lift the achievement, which means focusing on how students are taught and what they're taught. Are you okay with that?	He uses shared dissatisfaction to propose the need for a new type of theory of action—one that focuses on teaching. He directly asks whether there is agreement.
David	Yes, yes, so have you got a view in mind in terms of what's next?	

In this extract, Justin does not rebut David's externally focused explanations because, as he explains, their validity has not yet been checked. Rather, his critique suggests that an alternative focus on the curriculum and pedagogy is more likely to achieve the improvement they both seek. The acceptability of the alternative theory of action—one that focuses on what and how students are taught—is tested rather than assumed by directly asking David, "Are you okay with that?"

It is important to note that at this stage, Justin and David have yet to craft the details of what this alternative classroom-focused theory of action would look like. They have reached sufficient agreement, however, to motivate the search for a more effective alternative.

PHASE IV. IMPLEMENT AND MONITOR A NEW, SUFFICIENTLY SHARED THEORY OF ACTION

The major challenge for leadership in this fourth stage of the engagement process is to design and redesign the alternative theory so that it can be reliably implemented by all teachers without sacrificing the features that are essential to achieving improved outcomes. Mastering this challenge requires persistence and rich, real-time feedback about how the new theory of action is being implemented.

Use Implementation and Outcome Indicators

There are numerous excellent books on the inquiry and evaluation processes that help leaders monitor the progress of a planned change. One of the most useful is Bryk et al.'s (2015) book *Learning to Improve*—a book in which they stress the importance of measuring progress in order to "learn fast, fail fast and improve fast" (p. 173). Such rapid and ongoing learning helps leaders to adjust their new theory of action on the basis of frequent feedback about whether the critical indicators of improvement are at the required level. Those critical indicators should include measures of progress in implementation, as well as measures of progress in outcomes.

Too often, schools implement a program and only evaluate shifts in student outcomes after six months, a year, or even longer. I am currently working in a school whose senior leaders have decided, after a detailed review of a two-year investment in an externally facilitated math program, that their students' results have not shifted. While they had suspicions that the results were not as good as they had hoped, the lack of implementation indicators made it hard for them to persuade the external facilitators that all was not well. It also made it hard for them to establish the cause of the failure. Without such information, they don't know if the cause is variable teacher understanding of the program, variable implementation of its key teaching practices, inadequate support of teachers by the external facilitators, or a faulty program that will not deliver the promised results even if implemented with high fidelity.

If leaders are to "learn fast," they cannot wait for the next round of annual student testing to determine if the new literacy or math program is working. They need indicators of the quality and consistency of implementation, as well as indicators of shifts in the intended outcomes. Implementation indicators should provide them with feedback about such things as the following:

- At [a specified time], which teachers have adequate knowledge of the key concepts central to the new theory of action? Which teachers do not and need more support?
- At [a specified time], which teachers have largely positive attitudes toward the new theory of action, and which teachers still have concerns?
- At [a specified time], which teachers are using the new actions in their teaching, and which are not?

Notice that the monitoring of implementation is designed to identify the variation in implementation quality by attending to each teacher rather than to gloss over such variation by noting overall or average progress. More important than the average progress in teacher implementation of a new theory of action is the variability in such progress. Leading improvement requires careful attention to variation in implementation and outcomes, for it is the failure to reduce the wide variation in educational practice and outcomes that is the biggest obstacle to educational improvement. A student-centered leader wants every child to improve, not just those who happen to be taught by teachers who more readily change their practice. Early, respectful inquiry into why certain teachers are not using the new approach often reveals the need for better, more focused, or more context-specific learning opportunities. In my experience, poor-quality implementation is far more likely to be a matter of skill rather than of will. Leaders should address the variability in teacher practice using the same engagement process that I have described in this chapter. Check whether the teacher agrees that her students' results or attitudes are unsatisfactory, debate the relative merit of her current theory of action and the theory that you wish her to implement, address the factors that prevent implementation of the new theory, and continue to monitor progress in implementation and outcomes.

It is often hard to know the time at which it is reasonable to expect significant improvement in student results. Without implementation indicators, leaders can be convinced or convince themselves that positive results will come if they just wait a bit longer or invest a bit more. But hoping for the best is a professionally indefensible change strategy! More effective is to develop indicators for both implementation and outcomes that can be expected to show improvement within a far shorter time frame than the ultimate outcome indicators.

Embed the Indicators in the Work of Improvement

In this brief New Zealand case (Parr, Timperley, Reddish, Jesson, & Adams, 2006), I show how to establish and use implementation and outcome indicators that are closely aligned to the alternative theory of action. If leaders have gained agreement about the shifts in beliefs and actions that are required to implement a more effective theory, then clear indicators should be welcomed as a source of feedback and learning about whether teachers are making the agreed-upon shifts and whether the support they are receiving is adequate.

The case is based in a small rural elementary school that was participating in a literacy initiative designed to improve student writing. There was little difficulty gaining teachers' agreement that the writing results were problematic. Standardized test results, together with comparison of their students' work against year-level exemplars, showed the children to be well behind.

With the help of an external facilitator who had been trained to use the engagement approach, the beliefs and practices responsible for these unintended consequences were revealed. In essence, teachers believed, based on their earlier professional development, that the teaching of writing was largely a motivational exercise. This led them to spend considerably more time motivating writing than teaching how to write or letting students write on their own. Teachers were motivated to change, not only by the poor results in writing but also by feedback from students that indicated they did not understand the writing task well enough to monitor their own writing or learn from the feedback given by their teachers. These latter consequences were of particular concern to the teachers because they wanted their children to be self-regulated learners.

Over a period of four months, the facilitator worked with the principal, literacy leader, and teachers to develop, implement, and monitor a new theory of action for the teaching of recount writing. It is summarized in Figure 4.5.

Once the alternative theory of action is specified, as in Figure 4.5, it is a relatively small step to then develop a few practical indicators of shifts in beliefs, teacher actions, and student outcomes. Shifts in teacher beliefs were monitored by teacher ratings of their confidence in specifying the important learning objectives, making the success criteria clear for students, and providing feedback about writing in ways that supported students' further learning.

Teachers' Beliefs and Values

Students need to be explicitly taught how to write.

This requires being specific about what counts as good writing.

If taught well, students will develop confidence and competence as writers.

I have sufficient knowledge of and confidence in the teaching of writing to teach it well.

Teaching Actions for a Recount Writing Lesson

The teacher describes the learning objectives.

Success criteria are made explicit and illustrated.

Lesson activities are aligned to lesson aims.

The teacher's oral and written feedback is aligned with the success criteria.

Consequences

Children know the learning aims and success criteria for recount writing.

Children understand, from the teachers' feedback, what they need to be learning next.

Children enjoy writing.

Children make significant gains in writing achievement.

Teachers enjoy teaching writing.

Progress in implementing the actions described in Figure 4.5 was monitored by observing the extent to which teachers were able to incorporate the five actions in their writing lessons.

The consequences of the new approach for student learning were monitored by the facilitator and the teachers themselves asking students what they were supposed to be learning about writing, what the success criteria were for the type of writing they were doing, and what the teacher had told them about what to work on in their writing. The achievement outcomes were monitored through administration, four months after the baseline assessment, of the two assessment instruments used at the outset of the program.

Ideally, implementation and outcome indicators are embedded in the regular work of teaching and learning. Teachers inquire into student understanding as part of their lessons. Team and literacy leaders use the teaching indicators as part of their regular classroom observations, walk-throughs, or instructional rounds. Leaders administer and discuss quick confidence rating scales as part of their regular team meetings. Writing achievement data are gathered, analyzed, and discussed as part of the school's regular assessment cycle.

The point is not to complete a research project, get everything perfect, or drown in data. Rather, it is to get timely information that people agree is sufficiently trustworthy to use it to judge progress, identify unanticipated stumbling blocks, and make decisions about any needed revisions to the new theory of action.

● ● ● ● REFLECTION AND ACTION

1. In your experience, how do leaders typically justify the need for change? To what extent are they and you skilled in constructive problem talk?

2. Discuss, in your leadership team, how you can help one another to engage rather than bypass the theories of those who

initially oppose your proposal for improvement. Consider giving one another feedback about the extent to which you listened carefully, summarized each other's reasoning, and publicly checked the accuracy of your summary.

3. Does the culture in your team encourage respectful critique of each other's practice? How could you use this chapter to improve the quality and frequency of critique in the interest of improvement?

CHAPTER

5

Learning How to Lead Improvement: Coaching That Engages Principals

What opportunities do educational leaders have to learn how to lead improvement? How effective are those opportunities in teaching educational leaders the distinction between bypass and engage and in making the switch, when needed, from the former to the latter? More important still, how effective are those opportunities in demonstrating rather than just talking about how to engage others?

Increasing numbers of educational leaders experience some form of leadership coaching or its close cousin, mentoring. For example, Ontario's Ministry of Education invested $9.7 million just on mentoring new principals in a recent three-year period. In my own research on coaching (Robinson, 2016), I have been interested in the extent to which coaches engage or bypass the theory of action of the leaders they are coaching and the extent to which those leaders are taught how to switch, if needed, from bypass to engage in their own leadership of improvement.

It is very difficult to answer these questions because there is so little evidence available about what occurs in coaching sessions. I have been fortunate, however, through a research collaboration with colleagues at Vanderbilt University, to gain access to transcripts of coaching sessions in which coaches worked with principals over an eighteen-month period to build their capability as instructional leaders. The coaching was focused on learning from 360-degree evaluations of the principal's effectiveness in building trust and instructional leadership, and creating a strong school-wide academic focus. The key purpose of the coaching was to help principals to use the feedback to reduce important discrepancies between the survey findings and their desired levels of school and leadership performance.

In reviewing the transcripts, we came across one very skilled coach who worked with each of his principals to reveal, evaluate, and revise the tacit theories that prevented them from being more effective as instructional leaders. I have selected three extracts that demonstrate, through the actual words of this coach, how he engages rather than bypasses the thinking of his principals and challenges them to do the same with their teachers.

EXCERPT 1: ENGAGE OTHERS' THINKING

In this excerpt, the coach (Jared Stephens) is discussing with an elementary school principal (Delia) how to follow up with teachers on their instructional planning. Delia is concerned that some of her teachers are not correctly implementing the district's required Balanced Literacy (BL) program, including not using a word wall as recommended. She wonders what to do in the face of these teachers' objections.

Delia (principal):	So what if they say, "Well, we just really don't want to do that"? What . . . I mean, [the superintendent's] expectation is that we continue the Balanced Literacy in elementary.
Jared (coach):	Okay. So is there a way to do Balanced Literacy without using a word wall?
Delia:	It's an expectation.
Jared:	That was a great answer. It was not the question I asked.
Delia:	I know. I know. Yes, but not to the best, not . . .
Jared:	Do you know what their thinking is?
Delia:	I think their thinking—I don't really know, but I think their thinking is, okay, that kids, especially low-functioning kids, need a visual. Well, not just low-functioning . . .
Jared:	You're talking about what the District's thinking is.
Delia:	Yes.
Jared:	I'm asking you do you know what your teachers' thinking is?
Delia:	I have no idea.
[. . .]	
Jared:	What if the word wall got put up because they saw the value in it as opposed to being because you told them to put it up?
Delia:	Much more powerful because you're going to utilize it and how do you make that happen?
Jared:	Yeah.
Delia:	I think maybe going back to my original question and not saying, "Put up a word wall," but
	(Continued)

	"I noticed you all don't have a word wall and I noticed that there's not a lot of teaching charts on the wall." And there's not. I mean, it's like bare.
Jared:	Okay. If I ask you . . .
Delia:	And I just wonder why that was.
Jared:	Okay, let me frame for you a different way to think about that.
Delia:	Okay.
Jared:	"I'm a strong proponent of Balanced Literacy. Can you all talk to me a little bit about your understanding of what it means to use Balanced Literacy in your classroom? What are the key components of Balanced Literacy and why are those things so widely used? And let's have a conversation about Balanced Literacy."
Delia:	Gotcha.
Jared:	As opposed to, "I notice you're not doing this, you're not doing this, you're not doing this, you're not doing this."
Delia:	Okay. Okay.
Jared:	You see where I'm going?
Delia:	Yes. Yeah.
Jared:	Just from the standpoint of getting some sort of understanding of what they're thinking. They're making their thinking transparent.

In this example, engaging others means creating a dialogue between the thinking that drives Delia's approach to her teachers and the alternative approach suggested by her coach. Delia's theory illustrates the bypass approach to improvement, for she knows nothing of the thinking of her teachers; her focus is on the practices she wants her teachers to adopt, not on understanding their current practice. The coach's alternative theory is all about engagement; in his view, Delia needs to understand her teachers' beliefs about BL, articulate her own, and create a conversation between the two (Table 5.1).

Table 5.1 Analysis of Excerpt 1

Principal's current theory	Coach's alternative theory	Coach's interpersonal behavior	Analysis of coach's interpersonal behavior
1. The superintendent expects us to implement a Balanced Literacy (BL) program			
2. This expectation includes use of a word wall	Is it worth considering whether the word wall is an essential part of BL?	Direct inquiry about possibility of uncoupling BL and word wall Coach challenges P to provide her own views rather than those of the district	Coach engages with P's theory by revealing and challenging her taken-for-granted assumption about the necessity of the word wall Coach is beginning to challenge P's stance as an enforcer of district mandates
3. Use of a word wall is best BL practice		Coach appears to accept this evaluation	

(Continued)

Table 5.1 (Continued)

Principal's current theory	Coach's alternative theory	Coach's interpersonal behavior	Analysis of coach's interpersonal behavior
4. It is my job to ensure all teachers implement BL as required by the district	P should know her teachers' views about BL P should be promoting teachers' internal rather than external commitment to use of a word wall	Direct inquiry about her knowledge of teachers' views Coach evaluates P's answer as repeating district's views rather than giving teachers' views Coach repeats question about her knowledge of her teachers' views Coach evaluates P's stance as not promoting internal commitment Coach models how to inquire into the thinking of her teachers Coach compares his modeling with the negative evaluations P is communicating to her teachers	Coach's repeated questions interrupt her bypassing of her teachers' views Coach and P agree that internal commitment is desirable Coach models how to reframe P's bypass and enforcement stance into an engagement stance

The skill of this coach is multilayered, and it is important to unpick these layers in order to understand the type of facilitation and development opportunities that are required to build capability in engaging others when leading improvement.

Layer 1: The Coach Brings Relevant Knowledge

The first thing to notice is that the coach is not a tabula rasa, devoid of ideas, whose only role is to elicit the ideas of the principal. While helping the principal to make her tacit theory explicit is a key part of engagement, it also requires sharing one's own knowledge so that there is a dialogue between two theories. Even though those theories may be incomplete, evolving, and uncertain, the dialogue between them creates the possibility of reciprocal critique and a better shared theory. In summary, the first layer of this coach's skill is his relevant knowledge—knowledge that enables him to generate hunches ("Is she bypassing the thinking of her teachers?"), to formulate questions to check those hunches ("What do you know about the thinking of your teachers?"), and to provide evaluative standards (internal commitment is better than external commitment).

The coach brings relevant knowledge that enables him to

- generate hunches
- formulate questions to check on those hunches
- provide evaluative standards

Layer 2: The Coach Models How to Maintain a Shared Focus

The second layer of the coach's skill is his ability to ask direct questions, challenge the principal's thinking, and check his own understandings. But there is more to this layer than the presence of these interpersonal behaviors. Rather, his skill lies in his ability to focus these behaviors on those aspects of the principal's theory whose validity and utility are critical to achieving the leader's purpose. For example, the coach noticed that the principal was frustrated by some teachers' failure to implement word walls—a component of BL that she believed was essential. Since disagreement over this belief was a major source of her frustration, the coach directly inquired into its validity ("Is there a way to do BL without using a word wall?"). It is the application of interpersonal skills to the identification, evaluation, and revision of key beliefs that characterizes the skill of this coach. In short, it is not the presence or frequency of such behaviors as inquiry and challenge that is skillful but the ability of the coach to focus those behaviors on critical aspects of the principal's theory.

> In short, it is not the presence or frequency of such behaviors as inquiry and challenge that is skillful but the ability of the coach to focus those behaviors on critical aspects of the principal's theory.

Layer 3: The Coach Enacts the Interpersonal Values of Respect, Truth-Seeking, and Internal Commitment

The third and final layer of this coach's skill is his ability to enact the interpersonal values of respect, truth-seeking, and internal rather than external commitment—values that promote disclosure, trust, and reciprocal learning (Argyris & Schön, 1974, 1996). Those values are evident at two levels: in his interaction with the principal and in his modeling of how he wants her to engage with her teachers. The alignment of behavioral skill with the appropriate values is critical, for without those values, behaviors like inquiry and challenge can be enacted in closed- rather than open-minded ways. For example, inquiry can be leading rather than genuine, challenges can be rude rather than respectful, and advice can be imposed rather than offered. In Excerpt 1, the coach demonstrates respect for the principal through his repeated inquiry into her thinking and his persistence in gaining answers. Rather than give up on her when she misunderstands his questions, he treats her as capable of answering and of learning. As the principal's theory is made explicit, the second value of maximizing validity becomes important. This includes checking the accuracy of claims (e.g., about the necessity of the word wall), critiquing the soundness of her reasoning, and questioning whether her theory will enable her to reach her goals in principled ways. The third value of promoting internal commitment is seen in the coach's provision of choices and avoidance of imposition. For example, when the coach asks the principal for her reaction to teachers using word walls because they want to rather than because they are required to, he is checking that she shares his value of promoting internal rather than external commitment. The coach's ability to enact these three values means that his critique is unlikely to threaten the relationship he has with the principal.

EXCERPT 2: THE SELF-REFERENTIAL CRITIQUE

In Chapter 4, I explained the importance of using agreed-upon evaluative criteria when evaluating theories of action, as this avoids imposition of one's own values on others. A related way of avoiding imposition is to use self-referential critique—a type of critique that is based on values that are implicitly or explicitly endorsed by the person whose thinking is critiqued. Such critique could involve pointing out possible inconsistencies or checking whether the consequences of particular values are really as desirable as first thought. In Excerpt 2, Delia (principal) and Jared (coach) are discussing the feedback Delia has received from the last leadership survey recently completed anonymously by her teachers. Delia is frustrated by a comment made by a teacher about her instructional leadership. She believes she knows which teacher made the comment.

Delia (principal):	What evidence does she have that I don't observe classes and am not an instructional leader? What evidence does she have?
Jared (coach):	All right, can I ask you a question?
Delia:	Yeah.
Jared:	Okay. How much truth is in this statement?
Delia:	Not much.
Jared:	Okay, five minutes ago, you told me you needed to be in classes more.
Delia:	Yeah, but . . .
Jared:	Which fits? If I were . . .
Delia:	Okay.
Jared:	You see what I'm saying?
Delia:	Yeah.
Jared:	Tell me what you're feeling there. You want to be in classes more; somebody observed you, and they felt like you weren't in classes enough, so they're validating what you said.
Delia:	Right. Right, okay. I think what her thing is, or here's the untruth about it. There's truth in it, and then the untruth in it is I am in the classrooms of the ineffective teachers. That's what troubled me.
Jared:	She was not a classroom teacher for you?
Delia:	No. She was, the first year, and she was a stellar teacher.
Jared:	Yeah, I know she was a stellar teacher.
Delia:	So I wasn't in her room very often.
Jared:	Okay.
Delia:	That's her frame of reference.

Jared:	Right, exactly. You know, this was the conversation.
Delia:	But I was in the ineffective teachers' classrooms.
Jared:	Which she had absolutely no way to see.
Delia:	Yes.
Jared:	If she's in a classroom teaching, she had no way of knowing this.

Table 5.2 Analysis of Excerpt 2

Principal's current theory	Coach's alternative theory	Coach's interpersonal behavior	Analysis of coach's interpersonal behavior
The teacher's feedback is not based on evidence about how much I am in classrooms	The teacher's feedback is consistent with the principal's expressed desire to be in classrooms more than she currently is	Coach asks principal to reflect on the truth of the feedback Coach discloses his differing view of the feedback and the grounds for why he thinks it is fair Asks P why she felt teacher feedback was unfair	Coach engages with P's theory by using self-referential critique to challenge the validity of the principal's disagreement with her teacher's feedback
I am in the classrooms of the ineffective teachers	The teacher who gave the feedback is not ineffective and therefore did not see the principal visiting classrooms	Coach explains the perspective of the teacher and checks P's agreement with his analysis	Coach encourages P's engagement with teacher's thinking by taking teacher's perspective and then checking with P

The coach's self-referential critique interrupts the defensive response of the principal and enables her to consider the validity of the teacher's perspective. Together, coach and principal then craft a revised theory that is less oppositional and more likely to increase the principal's ability to learn from the survey feedback. Once again, the approach of the coach encourages the principal to engage with rather than bypass the perspective of her teachers.

> Together, coach and principal craft a revised theory that is less oppositional and more likely to increase the principal's ability to learn from the survey feedback.

How to Provide Self-Referential Critique

First, listen carefully to identify what the other person values or wants from the situation. Second, if you believe that the other person is acting in ways that are contrary to or inconsistent with what they value or want, say so, and explain why. Third, directly check whether the other person understands and agrees with your critique.

How to Provide Self-Referential Critique

1. Listen and identify your partner's values or wants
2. Articulate any inconsistencies you notice
3. Verify whether or not your observations are correct

EXCERPT 3: BYPASS AND REFRAMING

In this excerpt, Jared is talking with Carl, a principal who has asked for his help in holding more effective conversations with his teachers about improving the academic success of their students, many of whom come from economically disadvantaged families. Carl is frustrated with certain teachers whom he sees as making excuses for poor performance.

Carl (principal): You know this is hard for me. I don't want to hear excuses. You know. Don't tell me about how John has a miserable home life. Dad's not home—so what? We know that. When he comes to school, he's a regular kid. We teach him. He's here 7.5 hours. We bust it. We teach him 7.5 hours.

Jared (coach): He's an opportunity.

Carl: He's an opportunity.

Jared: Okay, here's my question to you. Every time you frame this to them, I encourage you not to frame it this way: "What more can we do?" "What more can we do?" Okay? Let me tell you what I think I hear in that, if I'm a teacher. I can't do any more, Mr. Roberts. I don't have any more time. So what's a way that you can reframe that question to get to the same thing you want to get to?

Carl: I could ask what strategies can we use, what— do you have any ideas? Do you all have any friends at other schools who are trying some of these strategies that are being successful?

Jared: You're still suggesting sort of the same thing. If you say to me, "Jared, in addition to your workload, I need you to give me a journal of all your thoughts and feelings tonight." Okay. It's probably not going to happen. But if you say to me, "You know, Jared, in lieu of turning in X, Y, and Z, I'd like you to spend that time doing a journal." And what we've done here is you've said to me, "This behavior is not important anymore because it's not getting the results we want. I'd like to substitute it, this for this." So instead of what more can we do, what behaviors can we change, what processes can we change, that doesn't cause us to have to do more but has us take

(Continued)

	a different look? Can we shift a lens and look at the problem differently? Do you see what I'm saying?
Carl:	Yeah.
Jared:	I want to be a part of that with you all. So you tell me the things that I'm doing that may be encumbering your ability to shift or [change]. Anything like that. Make it all fair game for conversation.
Carl:	Okay.
Jared:	Does that make sense?
Carl:	It makes perfect sense.

I have called this excerpt bypass and reframing because even though the coach describes the action component (add strategies) of the principal's theory of action, he does not inquire into and thus bypasses the beliefs that led Carl to use this strategy. Instead, he suggests a reframing of the actions (substitute rather than add) and uses self-referential critique to explain why he believes his alternative theory is preferable. In short, adding strategies will, he predicts, produce more of the excuses that the principal does not want to hear (Table 5.3).

When I elaborated the concept of bypass and engage in Chapter 3, I stressed that since bypass could produce positive outcomes, engagement was not always necessary. The critical question is whether Carl can adopt the coach's advice to substitute rather than add activities, without exploring his beliefs, **and that question is best answered by seeing what happens**. It may be that Jared's self-referential critique of Carl's approach, as inviting more excuses, and his reframing and modeling of the alternative substitute strategy is sufficient to enable Carl to adopt Jared's suggestion. If, however, Carl continues to lead change by asking his teachers for new ideas and obtains the same defensive responses, then Jared

Table 5.3 Analysis of Excerpt 3

Principal's current theory	Coach's alternative theory	Coach's interpersonal behavior	Analysis of coach's interpersonal behavior
The teachers are using students' home background as an excuse for their results			
I don't want to hear more excuses We have an opportunity to teach them for 7.5 hours per day		Listens to what the principal wants	
If I ask teachers for their ideas about successful strategies, they will become more committed to teaching these students	Teachers will interpret your brainstorming as asking them to do more, and that will trigger more excuses (e.g., lack of time)	Provides self-referential critique of P's theory and gives his reasons	Coach identifies P's strategies, bypasses his beliefs, and proposes alternative strategies with reasons
	It is more effective to reframe your approach from doing more to substituting for activities that are not working	Checks for P's reaction	
	P needs to open up the possibility that he may have contributed to the ineffective activities	Models how to introduce his suggested reframing and checks P's reaction	

should switch to an engagement approach. This would involve, in this example, asking why Carl believes that he will reduce the excuses and gain more commitment by seeking teachers' ideas and then collaboratively evaluating the validity of those beliefs.

Leadership coaching provides a powerful opportunity to teach educational leaders how to lead improvement by engaging rather than bypassing the theories in the practices they seek to influence. If coaches are to provide this opportunity, they need a complex set of knowledge and skills. Their knowledge provides the conceptual resources that enable them to predict the consequences of existing theories of action and to suggest alternative ones. Their interpersonal skills enable them to enact the values of respect, truth-seeking, and internal commitment so that the coach–leader relationship is strongly collaborative and focused on learning how to improve oneself and to support the learning of others.

● ● ● ● REFLECTION AND ACTION

1. Reflect individually or in a group about your experience of being coached. Identify and describe occasions in which the coach really enabled you to learn about your own leadership. What did the coach do that promoted your learning?

2. Reflect individually or in a group about your experience of being coached. What balance was struck between the provision of emotional support and learning? What were the consequences of the balance for your own leadership of improvement?

3. How are coaches selected and evaluated in your school or system? Discuss in a relevant group the implications of this chapter for the selection and evaluation of coaches.

CHAPTER
6

Learning How to Lead Improvement: Professional Learning That Engages Participants

Building the professional capability of teachers and leaders provides a powerful way of improving student learning and achievement. There is compelling evidence that investment in teacher and leader knowledge and skill has a far bigger effect on student outcomes than investment in such things as school architecture, computers, or extra staffing (Hattie, 2009).

Despite that generalization, teachers and leaders report having their time wasted at professional-learning events that are too theoretical, tell them what they already know, or are not well matched to the context in which they work. Researchers confirm that many professional-learning opportunities do not demonstrate the qualities required to change the practice of educators, let alone of the students they teach (Muijs et al., 2014). One of those qualities is engagement of the relevant existing understandings of those participating in the professional learning.

Teachers' prior knowledge and experience mean they invariably bring preconceptions about the topic to a professional-learning opportunity (Bransford, Brown, & Cocking, 2000). If those preconceptions conflict with the ideas they are being taught, and the conflict is bypassed, teachers may not be able to integrate the new ideas with their existing ones. Even young children bring powerful preconceptions, including misunderstandings, to their learning, so it is to be expected that the preconceptions of experienced adult learners are even more deeply held and felt. In the language of this book, this means that unless the new knowledge and skills are consistent with their existing theories of action, the learning required for improvement will not happen without engagement.

> Unless the new knowledge and skills [of professional learning] are consistent with [teachers'] existing theories of action, the learning required for improvement will not happen without engagement.

The relationship between learning and engagement has profound implications for the design of professional learning. The central consideration in the design of professional development that engages adult learners is how to provide resources and design activities that challenge their existing practice in ways that enable them to reach agreed-upon goals. In this chapter, I describe an opportunity I had to help a team design a professional-development experience that deeply engaged its participants. The process the team went through provides a detailed contrast between professional development that bypasses and engages the theories of action of learners.

THE CONTEXT

The Bastow Institute of Educational Leadership, part of the Victoria State Department of Education and Training in Australia, offers a rich range of leadership development opportunities to educational leaders across the state. Its leadership courses are designed by contractors, in collaboration with institute staff, school leaders, department officials, and consultants.

The state department of education had asked the institute to develop a course on principal health and well-being as part of its response to recent statewide surveys of principals that showed increasing levels of stress and job overload. Department officials were keen to be responsive to this evidence and to address growing concern among principal groups about role overload, stress, and access to effective support services.

In order to inform the department's response, officials commissioned or accessed a range of evidence-based reports about principals' well-being and use of time. The latter report, in particular, suggested that principals' choices about how to distribute leadership responsibilities and delegate tasks contributed to the overload and stress that they experienced. When principals attended initial presentations about these findings, some reacted with anger and resentment. It seemed, in their view, that they were being blamed for their own stress and role overload. What they wanted, instead of blame, was more resources and access to more timely and effective support. It was critical, therefore, that the design team plan a course that would be valued by the profession.

The course design team, made up of principals, departmental officials, industry experts, and course managers from the Bastow Institute, drafted a two-day course that comprised presentations from experts on resilience, work–life integration, delegation, and teamwork and culminated in the development of a personalized support plan.

It was at this stage that I was invited to join the design team and was briefed about the commissioned reports, initial reactions to those reports, and the work of the design team to date. My hunch was that while the commissioned reports had revealed some very interesting patterns of principal time use, too little attention had been given to the reasons for those patterns, and this had caused the rejection of some of their findings and recommendations. In short, my view was that the consultants had bypassed rather than engaged the theories of action that explained and sustained the principals' current patterns of time use, and it was possibly this bypass that had led to the rejection of some of the key findings in the reports. My job was to disclose and test this possibility and, if agreed, to help design a course that could truly engage principals' tacit theories about how to use their time.

In the following, I use the four phases of theory engagement (Figure 4.1) to tell the story of what happened after I joined the design team.

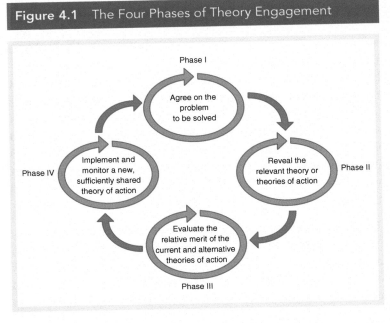

Figure 4.1   The Four Phases of Theory Engagement

PHASE I. AGREE ON THE PROBLEM TO BE SOLVED

As in most educational improvement efforts, there were several intersecting problems to be solved, and all had to be agreed on and investigated.

At the level of principal practice, we needed to agree that the problem to be solved was the declining levels of principal well-being and the unacceptably high levels of stress. While one course, in itself, could not solve this problem, we needed to agree that the eventual course design was fit for that purpose—with that purpose being to help principals gain greater control over their time and reduce their level of overload and stress.

At the level of the design team, I had to explain why I believed their current bypass approach to course design would not produce the intended behavioral changes in principals' patterns of time use and seek the designers' reactions to my beliefs.

Agreement on the problem of principal practice was quickly gained by asking each member of the design team to state the problem for which the course was part of the solution. Everyone expressed a similar view: the problem was the unacceptably high level of principal stress. We then aligned that problem with a set of intended learning outcomes for the course. By the end of the two days we wanted course participants to understand the factors that cause stress for principals in general and for each of them personally; understand the basis of their current decision making about time use and delegation; understand the impact of their current decisions about delegation and time use on their personal well-being; be aware of the available support services and able to advocate for any additional resources they required; and, finally, develop a personalized plan for their own health and well-being. Once we reached agreement about the intended outcomes of the course, the team used them as a touchstone against which to evaluate proposed changes to the course design.

Gaining agreement on the design problem was more complex, as before agreement could be reached, I needed to explain what I meant by *bypass* and *engage*, why I believed the former was problematic, and how the current draft design exemplified the bypass approach to improvement. The current course plan included 9.5 hours of input, over two days, from three different facilitators talking about well-being, resilience, social capital, and organizational design. Approximately 3.5 hours was planned over the two days for individual reflection and development of a personalized well-being plan. I argued that this input-driven course design was unlikely to enable participants to achieve the intended learning outcomes, as there was too little focus on the theories of action that explained principals' current patterns of time use. Since these patterns were long standing and likely to be deeply embedded in principals' beliefs about how to be an effective leader, they were unlikely to change without providing structured opportunities for participants to make these patterns explicit and examine their impact on principals' own well-being. Furthermore, principals' beliefs about how to do the job were likely to be the source of objections to the consultants' recommendations about how to control their workload by, for example, reducing their number of direct reports and increasing their delegation of tasks to other school leaders.

> The input-driven course design [placed] too little focus on the theories of action that explained principals' current patterns of time use. These patterns . . . were unlikely to change without providing structured opportunities for participants to make these patterns explicit and examine their impact on principals' own well-being.

In my view, a substantial part of the course needed to be devoted to teaching participants how to reveal, evaluate, and revise the theories of action that explained their current patterns of time use. Input from consultants should be treated as a resource for the critique and revision of principals' theories of action, and considerable time should be devoted to help principals with that difficult work. Course designers agreed that their current bypass approach may not make the intended impact and that it was worth experimenting with a different design.

In total, the process of agreeing on the principals' problem of time use and the problem with the draft course design took about three hours. From that point on, we focused on designing a course that would engage rather than bypass the theories of action that determined principals' current patterns of time use.

PHASE II. REVEAL THE RELEVANT THEORIES OF ACTION

Having agreed on the problems to be solved, the next phase of the design work involved identifying the tacit theory in principals' current practice. Two theories of action were constructed. The first was a general theory of action, based on the evidence found in the consultants' reports, about principals' typical patterns of time use, the beliefs that explained those patterns, and their consequences for principals' health and well-being (Figure 6.1). The second theory of action (Figure 6.2) was developed to illustrate how a personal theory of action could be developed for any particular principal.

Construct a General Theory of Action

By constructing Figure 6.1 together, the design team developed a shared understanding of the problem of practice we were trying to solve. We were also developing a resource that, if sufficiently accurate, would resonate with principals and give them confidence that we understood the challenges they would face in trying to shift their practice.

Figure 6.1 presents a highly generalized account of the theory of action that might partially explain principals' current patterns of time use. We began in the consequences box by giving due weight to the evidence in the consultants' reports that the principal's job was typically experienced as a paradoxical combination of high stress and high satisfaction.

Figure 6.1 A General Theory of Action for Principals' Time Use

Relevant Beliefs

1. Principals are servant leaders who should sacrifice their own time in order to protect teacher time.
2. Principals should protect teachers from unpleasantness (e.g., parental complaints).
3. Principals need to keep control as they are legally responsible for and accountable for everything in the school.
4. If principals do it themselves, they can be more confident it will be done well.
5. The system is unclear about what is reasonable to delegate.

Actions

On average . . .

1. Principals spend too little time on core improvement activities.
2. Principals spend considerable time on tasks such as
   a. Filling in and performing tasks for others
   b. Managing student behavior issues (e.g., suspensions and parental complaints)
   c. Personally managing infrastructure issues (e.g., buildings)
3. Principals spend widely variable amounts of their time on discretionary tasks (variation of 17 to 54 percent of time use). They
   a. Delegate less than their equivalent in other industries
   b. Consult widely on many issues
   c. Attend many meetings

Consequences

1. Decline in health and well-being indicators
2. High stress
3. Ninety-four percent of principals assessed as in overload

YET

4. High levels of satisfaction
5. Average of seven applicants for every Victorian principal position

Source: Evidence about the health, well-being, and satisfaction of Australian principals was drawn from Riley (2015).

The fact that there were, on average, seven applicants for every principal's position indicated that the job was, despite the stress, still attractive enough to ensure a field of applicants for vacant positions. At the same time, the decline in well-being and the fact that 94 percent of principals were judged to be overloaded on an objective measure could not be overlooked.

In completing the actions box of the template, we focused on identifying actions that might be causally implicated in the stress and overload and over which principals had some control. There was considerable evidence about those actions in a consultant's report regarding how much time principals allocated to over three hundred different tasks. The report showed that principals allocated widely varying times to the various task categories and that the variation could not be explained by school type or by the number and capability of those holding other leadership positions in the school. It was important, therefore, to probe further to discover what might explain why the average principal spent so much time in meetings and on tasks, like building maintenance, that they described as less important than core improvement activities like strategic planning and holding follow-up discussions with teachers after classroom observations.

Our suggested explanations for these actions are in the upper box labeled *relevant beliefs*. It is important to point out that beliefs are inclusive of systemic and contextual explanations of actions. Systemic factors are mediated through the perceptions and interpretations of actors; they do not operate independently of these subjective factors. The belief that the system is not clear about expected delegations may or may not be true. The point is that it is the *perception* of the system's lack of clarity, whether or not it is objectively true, that may help explain why principals are conservative in their delegation to others.

The beliefs operate as a set, interacting with each other to explain how principals use their time. For those principals who believe that self-sacrifice is an honorable part of servant leadership, their reluctance to delegate could be reinforced by a further belief that the system is unclear about what constitutes reasonable delegation. For those principals who have a high need to be in control, beliefs about being personally accountable for everything that happens in their school will reinforce their reluctance to delegate and will erode the time they have available for core improvement activities.

The point of Figure 6.1 was to provide the design team and, potentially, course participants themselves with a schematic account of the underlying reasons for principals' patterns of time use and some insight into what might be involved in shifting those patterns. It was now clear why a focus on principals' actions alone and recommendations to change them were unlikely to be effective. Explicit attention needed to be given to the beliefs that sustained those actions and that, together, contributed to the negative consequences.

> [Drafting Figure 6.1 revealed] why a focus on principals' actions alone . . . [was] unlikely to be effective. Explicit attention needed to be given to the beliefs that sustained those actions and that, together, contributed to the negative consequences.

Construct a Personal Theory of Action

The second personal theory of action (Figure 6.2) was based on an interview I conducted with Garry, a member of the design team who had experienced considerable stress in his first two years as principal and was now, as a facilitator, passionate about helping other principals avoid what he had been through. Even though now retired from what turned out to be a very successful principalship, he was able to vividly recall the beliefs and actions that had gotten him into trouble.

Although Garry wanted to be a strong instructional leader, he seldom got to issues of teaching and learning because he gave priority to the agendas of other people: parents, administrators, and misbehaving students. His highly reactive mode was explained by his belief that such responsiveness would build his own and the

Figure 6.2 A Personal Theory of Action for One Principal's Time Use

Relevant Beliefs

1. In order to be a good principal in this school, I need to respond personally and immediately to parents.

2. There is a tradition of such responding, and if I break it, I will lose goodwill.

3. I need to meet others' expectations of me, and quick responses to administrative requests are expected.

4. I will be evaluated negatively by my superiors if I'm seen as slow to respond to their requests.

5. Leading teaching and learning comes after the immediate administration is completed.

6. It is selfish to talk about my own needs and stress.

Actions

1. I spend . . .

   a. Thirty percent of my time on administrative tasks (e.g., compliance/occupational health and safety)

   b. Thirty percent of my time dealing with parents, phone calls, and staff issues, such as conflict between staff

   c. About 20 percent of my time managing student behavior issues

   d. Minimal time leading the improvement of teaching and learning

2. I answer about thirty to forty e-mails per day.

Consequences

1. I feel "like I'm in handcuffs" and have a high level of anxiety.

2. I feel overwhelmed and as if I'm going around in circles.

3. My sleep is poor.

4. I feel inadequate in the job, as I'm not leading teaching and learning.

5. I am liked, but the outcomes for students have not improved.

school's reputation with his superiors and the community and his tacit belief that others' agendas were more important than his own. The consequences for Garry were severe: sleepless nights, high levels of anxiety, and a feeling of inadequacy. The consequences for the school and its students were also serious; there was little improvement in teaching and learning. It was a colleague who eventually helped him to see the self-destructive nature of his beliefs and to make some much-needed personal and professional changes.

PHASE III. EVALUATE THE RELATIVE MERIT OF THE CURRENT AND ALTERNATIVE THEORIES OF ACTION

Once the design team had developed the two theories of action to explain current patterns of time use, our next step was to formulate alternative, more effective theories. Which action strategies needed to change in order to reduce the negative consequences produced by the current patterns of time use? What alternative actions were likely to be more effective? What changes in current beliefs and values were needed to support the changed actions?

Construct and Evaluate an Alternative General Theory of Action

Figure 6.3 presents a revised theory of action for principals' time use. The new suggested actions were largely drawn from the recommendations made by the consultants who studied principals' patterns of time use and their patterns of delegation. Implementation of the revised actions would require many principals to reorganize leadership positions in their school so as to reduce their number of direct reports, be more explicit about delegated responsibilities, and build leadership capability throughout the school.

Principals' priorities would need to shift from a reactive to a more proactive response to parental complaints and student

Figure 6.3 A General Alternative Theory of Action for Principals' Time Use

Beliefs and Values

1. An important part of a principal's job is to develop the leadership capability of others.

2. Leading collaborative improvement in teaching and learning is the core work of the principal.

3. A strategic principal is proactive rather than reactive.

4. Principals' health and well-being must be a high priority, as they can't lead effectively if they are unhealthy.

5. Principals are in charge of their own health and well-being.

On average, principals should . . .

1. reduce the number of staff they directly manage *by*

2. establishing clearly delegated responsibilities *and*

3. developing the leadership capabilities of their team *and*

4. acting strategically to identify and prevent the causes of repeated incidents such as parental complaints and student behavior issues and *thereby*

Actions

5. creating time for their leadership of the improvement of teaching and learning *and*

6. giving greater priority to their own professional development *and*

7. giving greater priority to their own health and well-being by accessing and advocating for appropriate forms of support.

Consequences

1. Increased trust of other leaders, a sense of teamwork, and reduced isolation

2. Faster progress in school improvement

3. Improved principal health and well-being (e.g., improved sleep, better family–work balance, increased self-efficacy, and greater job satisfaction)

4. Improved and better utilized health and well-being services

5. Principal role seen as more attractive and less stressful

management. These changes would allow more time for leading the improvement of teaching and learning and for their own professional and personal development.

A comparison of Figures 6.1 and 6.3 suggests the substantial shifts in principals' beliefs and values that are required if principals are to agree to trial the alternative theory. For many principals, adopting one or more of the recommended new actions would require significant reframing of their beliefs about how to be an effective principal. Sacrificing one's own agenda and needs in order to please others and fill gaps is not compatible with expecting others to take leadership responsibility and positioning oneself as a leader of leaders. Neither is taking charge of everything—because one does not trust others' capability—compatible with the explicit development of one's own and others' leadership.

The motivation for making such difficult shifts is, of course, the negative consequence of current patterns of time use. The shifts will not come immediately. After all, engagement is not about making a leap of faith. Rather, it is about agreeing that the alternative theory has sufficient merit that it is worth trying and monitoring the consequences.

Figure 6.3 is intended as a resource for all principals in the revision of their own personalized theories of time use. In Figure 6.4, I present Garry's revised theory of action. For him, the catalyst for change, in addition to his own stress and unhappiness, was the stark challenge he received from a colleague, who warned him of severe health consequences if he continued to do the job in his current fashion. Why, his colleague asked, was he giving such urgent attention to the streams of requests coming from the district and regional office? What did he think would happen if they were given lower priority or, in some cases, not responded to at all? The starkly contrasting attitude of his colleague to such requests challenged Garry's assumption that he had no option but to respond as he did. Clearly, that assumption was wrong, and alternative strategies were possible. Perhaps they were worth a try.

Relevant Beliefs

1. In order to be a good principal in this school, I need to develop strategies that prevent recurrent conflicts and crises.

2. By developing this proactive leadership, I grow my own reputation and that of the school.

3. I am more likely to be evaluated negatively by my superiors if the teaching and learning are poor than if I am tardy in responding to some administrative requests.

4. My own health and well-being are critical to the well-being of the school, and so I have a responsibility to look after myself and seek help.

Actions

1. I will spend . . .

   a. Thirty percent of my time developing the capability of my leadership team, including my own capability

   b. Thirty percent of my time on proactive, strategic leadership strategies to improve relationships with the community and establish a more positive behavior climate in the school

   c. About 20 percent of my time monitoring and discussing the improvement of teaching and learning

2. I will establish clear delegations and expect school leaders to address problems in their area of responsibility before coming to me.

3. I will delegate, postpone, and prioritize administrative tasks to ensure they do not take precedence over the tasks described above.

Consequences

1. I will feel more in control of my job, more satisfied, and less stressed.

2. The leadership team will be more trusting, more cohesive, and more capable.

3. The school's reputation will improve, with fewer complaints, a more positive culture, and improved behavior.

PHASE IV. IMPLEMENT AND MONITOR A NEW, SUFFICIENTLY SHARED THEORY OF ACTION

Having understood the concept of a theory of action and developed four examples, the design team reflected on the implications of this work for the design of the course they had been charged with developing. They were now clear that if the course was to engage rather than bypass the theory of action of participants, the primary role of the facilitators would change from that of providing input about resilience and well-being to supporting principals in the discovery, evaluation, and revision of the theory of action that explained their current patterns of time use. The consultants' reports and other research material were still critical, but they were now treated as resources for the discovery, evaluation, and revision of theories of action rather than as material to be presented and discussed.

The outcome of this reflection was collaborative construction by the design team of a radically different two-day schedule. The balance between the amount of time spent examining reports about other people's work and examining one's own practice shifted markedly. In the original design, the former was given three times as much course time as the latter. In the new design, this was reversed. Table 6.1 presents the revised schedule for the course that the design team developed and agreed to trial. The facilitators who were to lead the course expressed confidence that this design would be much more effective than their earlier one in helping principals to understand and reduce the sources of their stress and, in so doing, become more satisfied and more effective leaders of their schools.

Just as this book was going to press, I heard from Garry, a member of the design team and the principal featured in Figures 6.2 and 6.4. He had been hired by the Bastow Institute as a cofacilitator of the course, and his e-mail provided a rich account of what had happened when the course was trialed and first delivered. He wrote,

Table 6.1 A Course Design for Engaging Participants' Theory of Action

Course Components	Activities	Rationale
Precourse preparation	Self-assess own health and well-being using a provided tool	Participants arrive at the course having considered the health and well-being consequences of the way they currently do their job.
Day 1		
Psychological contract	Establish a psychological contract with participants: • Course is one strand of the system's response to concerns about principal health and well-being • Agree on intended learning outcomes of course • Focus is on their *own* practice • Ethical protocols and confidentiality Negotiate a safe way to share self-assessments and then share them	The psychological contract is important because course participants may not expect such an intense focus on their own practice, and so a safe environment is critical.
Key concepts and application	Explanation of theory of action and its components	These two figures about others' theories of action are resources for the development of their own theories of action.
	Discuss general theory of action (Figure 6.1) and its origins in various reports	
	Discuss personal theory of action (Figure 6.2)	

(Continued)

Table 6.1 (Continued)

Course Components	Activities	Rationale
Personal theories of action for current practice	Individuals make explicit their own current theory of action	
	Peer critique of the accuracy of the personal current theory of action is modeled by facilitator	
	Course participants then critique the accuracy of each other's drafts in pairs	Have the participants identified the actions and beliefs that drive the negative consequences of current practices?
Day 1 homework	• Each participant reflects on and revises his or her description of the theory of action that drives his or her current practice • Reading of resource material to inspire revision of their theory of action	
Day 2		
Resources for revision of current theory of action	Present and discuss resource material on how some principals overcome the job overload and personal stress they experience • Present research and recommendations on school design and delegation • Present research and recommendations on resilience strategies	Participants can actively consider relevance of resource material to the revision of their own theories.
	Facilitator models how this resource material informed the development of Figures 6.3 and 6.4	

Course Components	Activities	Rationale
Alternative theory of action	Participants develop an alternative theory of action that is intended to substantially reduce the negative and increase the positive consequences for their own health and well-being	Critique and feedback prevents trialing alternatives that do not address their problem.
	Peer critique of the effectiveness of the draft alternative theory of action is modeled by the facilitator	
	Course participants then critique the effectiveness of each other's drafts in pairs	
Action planning	An action plan is drafted to implement one or more of the actions described in the alternative theory	Sharing of action plans increases commitment and mutual support.
	Participants publicly commit to a follow-up process	

In December, we presented a three-hour "taster" prototype session to key stakeholders, and we ran into significant resistance. We skipped too quickly over the concept of engage versus bypass and its implications. Those who had been or were principals reacted strongly to what they perceived as blame shifting to principals during the first hour. By the end of the three hours, we had unanimous endorsement of the engage approach, but it was a rocky road at first.

In the actual two-day workshop, we couched our language far more carefully and spent more time teasing out the engage approach and preparing the participants for the

(Continued)

(Continued)

difference that was to come. There was no such resistance. But we did notice that the evaluations of the second day were even better than those of the first day, for by then, they had developed their alternative theory of action and were completely comfortable with the model of beliefs driving actions and resulting in sometimes unintended consequences. . . .

The workshop exceeded my expectations, and I was struck at the depth of reflection that occurred, especially around their beliefs and values and the recognition that there were alternative ways of thinking, acting, and being as a principal. . . .

You identified very accurately in the text how the role of the facilitators changes significantly in the *engage* model. I also present workshops on data literacy and school governance—but this was a very different beast both for us and for the participants.

I had wondered whether we could effectively alter long-held beliefs in a mere two-day workshop. I was immensely encouraged by what we saw and felt. It will be fascinating to revisit them in ten weeks' time to see what develops with their action plans. I suspect that real long-term change may occur for some participants. . . .

The superintendent, who didn't attend the workshop, rang me on Sunday to say he has never seen a course be referred to so regularly even after many days had gone by and how serious people were with their action plans.

The concepts of *bypass* and *engage* have profound implications for the design and delivery of professional learning. When the intended outcome is change in practice, a bypass approach to course design and delivery will produce single-loop change at best. Course participants will select those resources, ideas, and recommendations that fit their current style and belief systems. If aspects of their style and belief system are implicated in the problem, then a bypass approach will not produce improvement. If the problem requires transformative, double-loop learning and change, an engagement approach is needed with facilitators who are skilled in helping participants make the links between the problems they are trying to solve, the actions that are contributing to them, and the beliefs and values that explain those actions. Making these links is a far cry from the usual approach of presenting material and asking participants to "apply it" to their own practice. Such instructions assume that the material is applicable and leave participants to do the hardest part of all—to figure out how to integrate new practices into their existing theories of action. It is no wonder that any perceived tension between the old and the new triggers reactions like, "It won't work in my context," or, "I've tried that, and it doesn't work," or, "In our system, that would be impossible."

Does this mean that *all* professional learning should be designed to engage rather than bypass theories of action? If the goal is to present new information and ideas, then the bypass approach is appropriate. As I discussed in Chapter 3, bypass approaches to improvement can work when the content of a course is sufficiently compatible with the current theories of practice of participants. However, when there is significant tension between the two, deeper, more transformative learning is required, and that involves engaging rather than bypassing the current theories of action of participants.

> How can you tell which approach is required—bypass or engage? Get early feedback about your planned approach. If there is misunderstanding of or opposition to your ideas, then use the engagement approach.

How do you tell which approach is required? Leaders can tell quite quickly by getting early feedback about their planned approach. If there is misunderstanding of or opposition to their ideas, then the engagement approach is required. The key is to listen carefully and value the pushback rather than to downplay it or explain it away.

A leader must listen and be ready at any time and for any aspect of an improvement process to switch from bypass into engagement mode, whether it be for a few deep conversations or, as in this case, for most of the design process.

● ● ● ● REFLECTION AND ACTION

1. Discuss the design of your most recent professional learning and whether it achieved the intended improvement. Do the concepts of bypass and engage help explain the degree to which the intended improvement was achieved?

2. Identify a future professional-learning opportunity that is being offered by your team, school, or district. If the goal is improved practice, how could you design that learning to ensure engagement rather than bypass of participants' current theories of action?

Afterword

By Stephen Dinham

There is a tension between change and improvement. How much change can occur within a "comfort zone"—that is, to what extent can doing more of the same with the status quo result in improvement, without the introduction of potentially disruptive change? How much change is too much change? How important is change management? How significant are barriers arising from previous unsuccessful attempts at change? To what extent can noncore mandated change undermine or distract attempts at core change in education? These are important questions, but what is clear is that educators have experienced waves of sometimes contradictory change over decades, making new attempts at change, even those generated by educators themselves, problematic.

The vast majority of educators genuinely want to improve teaching and learning, yet many feel overwhelmed. Principals struggle to keep their focus on instructional leadership in the face of mounting administrative and accountability mandates. New school leaders, in particular, struggle to be effective when faced with superficial professional learning opportunities, numerous standards, and multiple initiatives. System leaders feel similar pressure from governments and broader society. Pressure for improvement of student outcomes thus comes from both within and outside the school, and is increasing.

This book by Viviane Robinson addresses these significant questions and provides wise, practical, logical, grounded, evidence-based counsel and direction to assist educational leaders in an environment in which they are under pressure to make rapid and significant improvements. In particular, Robinson advocates and demonstrates the importance of educational leaders actively engaging with (and not merely instigating), monitoring, and evaluating change. This "leading from the front" is essential, both symbolically and practically, in my experience, if change is to be successful.

Robinson rejects the mechanistic, linear, "shopping list" view of change by underlining the importance of leaders working with and through other people to change what they know, can do, and even believe and value. The engagement of leaders with those involved with change is essential if change—and we are essentially talking about improvement in student outcomes, broadly defined as academic, personal, and social—is to be effective and sustainable.

Robinson equates improvement with a positive impact on learners. This is particularly pleasing because there is still far too much educational research that divorces leadership from teaching, and teaching from learning.

A highly experienced and respected international researcher and expert in the field of educational leadership, Robinson offers a comprehensive examination, explication, and illustration of the change improvement process in education. Her book is logically developed from foundation principles to take the reader through the thinking, understanding, planning, professional-learning, action, and evaluative processes. The use of general and personal theories of action is appropriate and effective. The work is supported well by illustrations and extracts from actual cases of aspects of change. **I think its greatest strength is the emphasis throughout on working with and through other people and the interpersonal and cognitive work this requires**. *Reduce Change to Increase Improvement* provides a timely and valuable resource for building our understanding of and capability in making the changes that make a difference to students.

Stephen Dinham
Associate Dean (Strategic Partnerships) and
Professor of Instructional Leadership
Melbourne Graduate School of Education
University of Melbourne, Australia

References

Argyris, C., & Schön, D. A. (1974). *Theory in practice: Increasing professional effectiveness.* San Francisco, CA: Jossey-Bass.

Argyris, C., & Schön, D. A. (1996). *Organizational learning II: Theory, method and practice.* Reading, MA: Addison Wesley.

Bransford, J. D., Brown, A. L., & Cocking, R. R. (Eds.). (2000). *How people learn: Brain, mind, experience, and school* (Expanded ed.). Washington, DC: National Academy Press.

Bryk, A. S., Gomez, L. M., Grunow, A., & LeMahieu, P. G. (2015). *Learning to improve: How America's schools can get better at getting better.* Cambridge, MA: Harvard Education Press.

Bryk, A. S., Sebring, P. B., Allensworth, E., Luppescu, S., & Easton, J. Q. (2010). *Organizing schools for improvement.* Chicago, IL: University of Chicago Press.

Caygill, R. (2013). *Mathematics: Year 5 students' mathematics achievement in 2010/11: New Zealand results from the Trends in International Mathematics and Science Study (TIMSS).* Wellington, NZ: Ministry of Education.

Chamberlain, M. (2007). Mathematics and science achievement in New Zealand: Summing up New Zealand's participation in three cycles of TIMSS at year 9. Wellington, NZ: Ministry of Education, Research Division.

City, E. A., Elmore, R. F., Fiarman, S. E., & Teitel, L. (2009). *Instructional rounds in education: A network approach to improving teaching and learning.* Cambridge, MA: Harvard Education Press.

Cohen, D. K., & Mehta, J. D. (2017). Why reform sometimes succeeds: Understanding the conditions that produce reforms that last. *American Educational Research Journal.* doi:10.3102/0002831217700078

Elmore, R. F. (2004). *School reform from the inside out: Policy, practice, and performance.* Cambridge, MA: Harvard Education Press.

Hattie, J. (2009). *Visible learning: A synthesis of over 800 meta-analyses relating to achievement.* London, UK: Routledge.

Hunter, R. (2010). Changing roles and identities in the construction of a community of mathematical inquiry. *Journal of Mathematics Teacher Education, 13*(5), 397–409.

Leithwood, K., Harris, A., & Hopkins, D. (2008). Seven strong claims about successful school leadership. *School Leadership & Management, 28*(1), 27–42.

Mourshed, M., Chijioke, C., & Barber, M. (2010). *How the world's most improved school systems keep getting better.* London, UK: McKinsey & Company.

Muijs, D., Kyriakides, L., van der Werf, G., Creemers, B., Timperley, H., & Earl, L. (2014). State of the art—Teacher effectiveness and professional learning. *School Effectiveness and School Improvement, 25*(2), 231–256.

Park, V. (2008). *Beyond the numbers chase: How urban high school teachers make sense of data use* (Doctoral dissertation). University of Southern California, Los Angeles.

Parr, J., Timperley, H., Reddish, P., Jesson, R., & Adams, R. (2006). *Literacy professional development project: Milestone 5* (Final Report). Wellington, NZ: Learning Media. Retrieved from http://www.educationcounts.govt.nz/publications/literacy/16813

Pink, D. H. (2009). *Drive: The surprising truth about what motivates us.* New York, NY: Riverhead Books.

Prochaska, J. O., DiClemente, C. C., & Norcross, J. C. (1992). In search of how people change: Applications to addictive behaviors. *American Psychologist, 47*(9), 1102–1114.

Riley, P. (2015). *The Australian principal occupational health, safety and wellbeing survey, 2015.* Institute for Positive Psychology and Education, Australian Catholic University, Fitzroy, Victoria, Australia.

Robinson, V. M. J. (2011). *Student-centered leadership.* San Francisco, CA: Jossey-Bass.

Robinson, V. M. J. (2014a). Single and double loop learning. In D. Phillips (Ed.), *Encyclopedia of educational theory and philosophy* (pp. 754–756). Thousand Oaks, CA: Sage.

Robinson, V. M. J. (2014b). Theories of action. In D. Phillips (Ed.), *Encyclopedia of educational theory and philosophy* (pp. 807–810). Thousand Oaks, CA: Sage.

Robinson, V. M. J. (2016). Reciprocal coaching: Learning the lessons from research. *Principal Connections, 20*(1), 18–20.

Robinson, V. M. J., Lloyd, C., & Rowe, K. J. (2008). The impact of leadership on student outcomes: An analysis of the differential effects of leadership type. *Educational Administration Quarterly, 44*(5), 635–674.

Robinson, V. M. J., & Timperley, H. S. (2007). The leadership of the improvement of teaching and learning: Lessons from initiatives with positive outcomes for students. *Australian Journal of Education, 51*(3), 247–262.

Robinson, V. M. J., & Timperley, H. S. (2013). School improvement through theory engagement. In M. K. Lai & S. Kushner (Eds.), *A developmental and negotiated approach to school self-evaluation* (Vol. 14, pp. 163–177). Bingley, England: Emerald Group Publishing Ltd.

Robinson, V. M. J., & Walker, J. C. (1999). Theoretical privilege and researchers' contribution to educational change. In J. S. Gaffney & B. J. Askew (Eds.), *Stirring the waters: The influence of Marie Clay* (pp. 239–259). Portsmouth, NH: Heinemann.

Schmidt, W. H., Burroughs, N. A., Zoido, P., & Houang, R. T. (2015). The role of schooling in perpetuating educational inequality: An international perspective. *Educational Researcher, 44*(7), 371–386.

Sinnema, C. E. L., Le Fevre, D., Robinson, V. M. J., & Pope, D. (2013). When others' performance just isn't good enough: Educational leaders' framing of concerns in private and public. *Leadership and Policy in Schools, 12*(4), 301–336.

Slater-Brown, K. (2016). *Ability grouping in mathematics: We know it is not an equitable practice, so why are we doing it?* (Unpublished master's thesis). University of Auckland, New Zealand.

Slavin, R. (2017, February 2). Transforming transformation (and turning around turnaround). *Huffington Post.* Retrieved from http://www.huffingtonpost.com/entry/transforming-transformation-and-turning-around-turnaround_us_5893b09be4b02bbb1816b8aa

Spiegel, J. S. (2012). Open-mindedness and intellectual humility. *Theory and Research in Education, 10*(1), 27–38.

Timperley, H. S., Wilson, A., Barrar, H., & Fung, I. (2007). *Teacher professional learning and development: Best Evidence Synthesis Iteration.* Wellington, New Zealand: Ministry of Education. Retrieved from https://www.educationcounts.govt.nz/publications/series/2515/15341

Zimmerman, J. (2006). Why some teachers resist change and what principals can do about it. *National Association of Secondary School Principals Association Bulletin, 90*(3), 238–249.

Index

Argyris, C., 14, 17, 19, 20

Balanced Literacy program
example, 72–77,
75–76 (table)
Barrar, H., 7
Bastow Institute of Educational
Leadership, 89
Bryk, A. S., 2, 5, 64
Bypass approach, xvi, xviii,
25–27, 26 (figure)
alternative theory, critical
scrutiny of, 29
critical evaluations and,
60–61, 60 (figure)
double-loop learning,
lack of, 28
invisible beliefs/values
and, 27
judgmental leadership
and, 56
large-scale reform efforts
and, 30–32
limitations of, 28–29
mutual mistrust,
development of, 29
New Zealand national
reform example of,
30–32
outcomes of, 26 (figure), 28
persuasive process and,
26 (figure), 27–28,
37–38

professional development
opportunities and,
92–93, 106–107
single-loop learning and, 28
See also Engagement
approach; Engaging
professional
development;
Improvement

Change, 1
comfort zones and, 109
disruptive/costly process of,
5–6, 109
educational reform, impact
on learners and,
xvii, 6–8
effectiveness evaluation and,
5, 6, 7–8
frequency of, xv
guiding questions for, 109
implementation, complexity
of, xv, 13–14
improvement, positive
educational impact
and, 6–8
improvement vs. change
and, 2, 3–6, 109
ineffective change and, xv,
xvi, 1–2, 4, 6, 11
intended improvement,
structures/processes for,
xvii, 3–4, 5, 6

leader accountability/
responsibilities and, 3–5
payoff of, xv, 1, 2
process of change and,
xv, 4–5
program design/evaluation
and, 2–3, 4
resistance to, 1, 5, 54–55
single-/double-loop learning
and, 20–22, 21 (figure)
uncertainty and, 5
undesirable change
and, 2–3
See also Bypass approach;
Change leadership;
Engagement approach;
Improvement;
Improvement
challenges; Innovation
Change leadership, xv, 1
accountability/
responsibilities of, 3–5
appreciation of underlying
theories and, 35
barriers to implementation
and, 28
bypass approach and, xvi
change process and, xv
change vs. improvement
and, 2, 3–6
collective inquiry process
and, 4–5, 8
effectiveness evaluation
and, 8
engagement approach and,
xvi–xviii
implementing agents,
perspective of, xvi, 5–6
improvement, positive
educational impact
and, 6–8
indicators of improvement
and, 7–8
ineffective change and, 11
intended improvement,
structures/processes for,
xvii, 3–4

international student
achievement data
and, 8
logic of change,
development/
communication of, 3–4
moral purpose of education
and, 6–7, 8
project milestones, timely
completion of, 7
quality of leadership
and, 9
stakeholders, consultation
with, xvi, 4
status quo, dissatisfaction
with, xvii
student-centered leadership
and, 11
systems-level improvement
efforts and, 8–9
teachers' practice/attitudes,
change in, 7–8, 14
theories of educational
leadership and, 9
theories of improvement,
development of, 4–5
undesirable change
and, 2–3
See also Bypass approach;
Change; Coaching
for improvement;
Engagement approach;
Engaging professional
development; Ethics
issues; Improvement
Coaching for improvement,
71–72
Balanced Literacy
implementation
example of, 72–77,
75–76 (table)
bypass approach, reframing
and, 82–86, 85 (table)
coaching session
transcripts, 72
internal commitment
and, 78–79

others' thinking,
engagement of, 72–77,
75–76 (table)
positive interpersonal
values, enactment of,
78–79
relevant knowledge,
provision of, 77
self-referential critique and,
79–82, 81 (table), 84
shared focus, modeling of,
77–78
theory of action, bypass/
engagement approaches
and, 72, 86
360-degree evaluations
and, 72
truth-seeking and, 78–79
See also Change leadership;
Engagement approach
Communities of learners, 3–4
Constructive problem talk,
40–43, 42 (table)

Defensive problem talk, 43–45
Double-loop learning, 20–22,
21 (figure), 28

Engagement approach, xvi,
25–27, 26 (figure)
appreciation of underlying
theories and, 35
collective/reciprocal process
and, xvii, 4–5, 29, 33,
35, 38
critical evaluations and,
61–62, 62 (figure)
dialogical process and,
25–27, 26 (figure)
four-phase model, repeated
cycles of, xvii
implementation process
and, 28, 29, 32–33
interim evaluation of theories
and, 26 (figure), 27, 33
interpersonal challenges in,
xvii–xviii, 27

new practices, integration
of, xvi–xvii
outcomes of, 26 (figure), 27
Phase I/agreement on
fundamental problem
and, 91–93
Phase II/inquiry into
relevant theories of
action and, 93–98
Phase III/evaluate current
and alternative theories
of action and, 98–101
Phase IV/implement and
monitor new shared
theory of action and,
102–108
professional development
opportunities and,
88–89, 93, 107–108
school-wide initiative
example of, 33–35
status quo, dissatisfaction
with, xvii, 33, 39–40
student achievement and,
87–88
tacit theory, inquiry
into, 27
trust, development of,
4, 38
See also Bypass approach;
Change; Change
leadership; Coaching
for improvement;
Engaging professional
development;
Four-phase model of
theory engagement;
Improvement;
Innovation
Engagement Model. *See*
Four-phase model of
theory engagement
Engaging professional
development, 17,
87–88
alternative general theory
of action, construction/

evaluation of, 98–100,
99 (figure)
alternative personal theory
of action, construction/
evaluation of, 100,
101 (figure)
Bastow Institute of
Educational Leadership
context and, 89–90
bypass approach and, 92–93,
106–107
design of professional
learning and, 88–89,
91–92, 102,
103–105 (table)
engagement approach and,
88–89, 93, 107–108
four-phase model of theory
engagement summary
and, 90, 90 (figure)
general theory of action,
construction of, 93–96,
94 (figure)
ineffective professional-
learning events and, 88
learning-engagement
relationship,
implications of, 88–89,
107–108
personal theory of action,
construction of, 96–98,
97 (figure)
Phase I/agreement on
fundamental problem
and, 91–93
Phase II/inquiry into
relevant theories of
action and,
93–98
Phase III/evaluate current
and alternative theories
of action and, 98–101
Phase IV/implement and
monitor new shared
theory of action and,
102–108

prototype session,
presentation of,
105–106
student achievement and,
87–88
teachers' prior knowledge,
preconceptions
and, 88
theories of action, new
knowledge/skills and,
88, 89, 92
See also Coaching for
improvement
Espoused theories, 18,
18 (figure), 19, 27
Ethics issues:
change process and, xv
moral purpose of education
and, 6–7, 8

Four-phase model of theory
engagement, xvii, 37
alternative theories,
evaluation/design of,
59, 64
constructive problem
talk and, 40–43,
42 (table)
continuous improvement,
ethos of, 40–41
critical evaluations, bypass
approach and, 60–61,
60 (figure)
critical evaluations,
engagement approach
and, 61–62,
62 (figure)
data analysis, role of, 40
defensive problem talk and,
43–45
direct/respectful evaluations
and, 62–64, 63 (table)
direct/respectful questions
and, 46–49, 47–48 (table)
engaging theories of action
and, 37–38

evaluation criteria,
    agreement on, 57–59
evaluation of theories,
    postponement of, 49–50
    guiding questions for
    inquiry and, 46
implementation quality,
    variations in, 65–66
improvement, critical
    indicators of, 64–66
improvement work,
    embedded indicators
    and, 66–69, 68 (figure)
interpersonal challenges,
    evaluation phase and,
    59–62, 60 (figure),
    62 (figure)
iterative cycle of, xvii, 38
leading improvement,
    evaluative nature of,
    55–56
Phase I/agreement on
    fundamental problem
    and, 38–45
Phase II/inquiry into
    relevant theories of
    action and, 45–55
Phase III/evaluate current
    and alternative theories
    of action and, 55–64
Phase IV/implement and
    monitor new shared
    theory of action and,
    64–69
phases, summary of, 38,
    39 (figure)
resistance to change and,
    54–55
status quo, shared
    dissatisfaction with,
    39–40
theory of action
    components, systematic
    inquiry into, 50–55,
    51–53 (table), 54 (figure)
trust, development of, 38, 41

values of importance,
    identification of, 56–57
weak motivators for change
    and, 39
See also Engagement
    approach; Engaging
    professional
    development; Theories
    of action
Fung, I., 7

Gomez, L. M., 2, 5, 64
Grunow, A., 2, 5, 64

Implementing agents, xvi, 5–6,
    29, 32–33, 55
See also Bypass approach;
    Change leadership;
    Engagement approach
Improvement, xv
    bypass approach to, xvi,
    xviii
    change vs. improvement
    and, 2, 3–6
    current practice, influences
    on, xvi
    engagement approach to,
    xvi–xviii
    future-focused agenda
    and, xvi
    implementing agents,
    perspective of, xvi
    indicators of, 6–8
    ineffective change and, xv,
    1–2, 4, 6
    intended improvement,
    structures/processes for,
    xvii, 3–4, 5, 6
    leadership quality
    and, 9
    moral purpose of education
    and, 6–7, 8
    new practices, integration
    of, xvi–xvii
    positive educational impact
    and, 6–8

proxy indicators of, 7–8
school self-management
reform and, 3–4
teachers' practice/attitudes,
change in, 7–8
theories of improvement,
development of, 4–5
See also Bypass approach;
Change; Change
leadership; Coaching
for improvement;
Engagement approach;
Engaging professional
development; Ethics
issues; Improvement
challenges; Innovation
Improvement challenges, 13
change, implementation
complexities and, xv,
13–14
single-/double-loop learning
and, 20–22, 21 (figure)
spelling program
implementation
example, 21–22
See also Bypass approach;
Change; Change
leadership; Coaching
for improvement;
Engagement approach;
Engaging professional
development;
Improvement; Theories
of action
Innovation, 1
change vs. improvement
and, 1–2
early adopters and, 1
enthusiasm about, 1
technology, integration of, 1
See also Change;
Engagement approach;
Improvement
Integrated practices, xvi–xvii
Interim evaluation,
26 (figure), 27

International student
achievement data, 8

Leadership. *See* Change
leadership; Coaching for
improvement;
Engaging professional
development
LeMahieu, P. G., 2,
5, 64
Lloyd, C., 11

Numeracy initiative, 2–3

Park, V., 40
Pink, D. H., 37
Problems. *See* Constructive
problem talk; Defensive
problem talk;
Four-phase model of
theory engagement
Professional development
opportunities, 17
See also Coaching for
improvement;
Engaging professional
development

Riley, P., 94
Robinson, V. M. J., 9, 11
Rowe, K. J., 11

Schön, D., 14, 17, 19, 20
Single-loop learning, 20–22,
21 (figure), 28
Sound Waves spelling
program, 21
Student achievement:
change vs. improvement
and, 2, 3–6
educational leadership,
impact of, 8–11,
10 (figure)
See also Change; Change
leadership; Engagement
approach; Improvement

Student-centered
  leadership, 11
  dimensions of leadership
    effects and, 9–10,
    10 (figure)
  student outcomes, impact
    on, 8–11, 10 (figure)
  educational reform, impact
    on learners and, xvii,
    8–11, 10 (figure)

Teaching practices:
  change process and, 7–8, 14
  professional development
    opportunities and, 17
  teacher's prior knowledge
    and, 88
  See also Change; Change
    leadership; Coaching
    for improvement;
    Engaging professional
    development;
    Improvement;
    Improvement
    challenges; Theories of
    action
Theories in use, 17–19,
  18 (figure), 27
  See also Theories of action
Theories of action, 14
  change leaders, insight
    of, 17
  change process and, 15, 17,
    19, 20–22, 21 (figure)
  components of, 14–15,
    15 (figure), 19
  espoused/in-use theories,
    mismatch between, 19
  espoused theories
    and, 18, 18 (figure),
    19, 27
  future theories of action
    and, 14–17, 16 (figure)

general theory of action,
  construction of, 93–96,
  94 (figure)
improvement strategy,
  design of, 19, 20
opportunities for
  improvement and, 17
personal theory of action,
  construction of, 96–98,
  97 (figure)
proposed changes, reactions
  to, 17
single-/double-loop learning
  and, 20–22, 21 (figure)
theories in use and, 17–19,
  18 (figure), 27
units of analysis and, 15, 21
  See also Bypass approach;
  Engagement approach;
  Engaging professional
  development;
  Four-phase model
  of theory engagement;
  Improvement challenges
Theory engagement. See
  Engagement approach;
  Engaging professional
  development;
  Four-phase model of
  theory engagement
THRASS spelling program, 21
Timperley, H. S., 7
Trends in International
  Maths and Science Study
  (TIMSS), 2
Trust, 4, 29, 38, 41

Victoria State Department of
  Education and Training, 89

Wilson, A., 7
Words Their Way spelling
  program, 21

CORWIN
LEADERSHIP

 Simon T. Bailey & Marceta F. Reilly
On providing a simple, sustainable framework that will help you move your school from mediocrity to brilliance.

 Edie L. Holcomb
Use data to construct an equitable learning environment, develop instruction, and empower effective PL communities

 **Debbie Silver & Dedra Stafford**
Equip educators to develop resilient and mindful learners primed for academic growth and personal success.

 **Peter Gamwell & Jane Daly**
A fresh perspective on how to nurture creativity, innovation, leadership, and engagement.

 **Steven Katz, Lisa Ain Dack, & John Malloy**
Leverage the oppositional forces of top-down expectations and bottom-up experience to create an intelligent, responsive school.

 **Lyn Sharratt & Beate Planche**
A resource-rich guide that provides a strategic path to achieving sustainable communities of deep learners.

 **Peter M. DeWitt**
Meet stakeholders where they are, motivate them to improve, and model how to do it.

Leadership that Makes an Impact

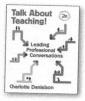

Charlotte Danielson
Harness the power of informal professional conversation and invite teachers to boost achievement.

Liz Wiseman, Lois Allen, & Elise Foster
Use leadership to bring out the best in others—liberating staff to excel and doubling your team's effectiveness.

Eric Sheninger
Use digital resources to create a new school culture, increase engagement, and facilitate real-time PD.

Russell J. Quaglia, Michael J. Corso, & Lisa L. Lande
Listen to your school's voice to see how you can increase engagement, involvement, and academic motivation.

Michael Fullan, Joanne Quinn, & Joanne McEachen
Learn the right drivers to mobilize complex, coherent, whole-system change and transform learning for all students.

CORWIN LEADERSHIP

A SAGE Publishing Company

Helping educators make the greatest impact

CORWIN HAS ONE MISSION: to enhance education through intentional professional learning.

We build long-term relationships with our authors, educators, clients, and associations who partner with us to develop and continuously improve the best evidence-based practices that establish and support lifelong learning.

Solutions you want. Experts you trust. Results you need.

AUTHOR CONSULTING

Author Consulting

On-site professional learning with sustainable results! Let us help you design a professional learning plan to meet the unique needs of your school or district. www.corwin.com/pd

INSTITUTES

Institutes

Corwin Institutes provide collaborative learning experiences that equip your team with tools and action plans ready for immediate implementation. www.corwin.com/institutes

ECOURSES

eCourses

Practical, flexible online professional learning designed to let you go at your own pace. www.corwin.com/ecourses

READ2EARN

Read2Earn

Did you know you can earn graduate credit for reading this book? Find out how: www.corwin.com/read2earn

Contact an account manager at (800) 831-6640 or visit **www.corwin.com** for more information.